Battlegroun...

LOOS – HILL 70

Battleground Europe

LOOS – HILL 70
The South

Andrew Rawson

Series Editor
Nigel Cave

LEO COOPER

First published in 2002 by
LEO COOPER
an imprint of
Pen & Sword Books Limited
47 Church Street, Barnsley, South Yorkshire S70 2AS

Copyright © Andrew Rawson
ISBN 0 85052 904 2

Printed by CPI UK.

*For up-to-date information on other titles produced under the Leo Cooper imprint,
please telephone or write to:*

Pen & Sword Books Ltd, FREEPOST, 47 Church Street
Barnsley, South Yorkshire S70 2AS
Telephone 01226 734222

CONTENTS

Introduction by Series Editor

For some years now I have been looking for an author to extend the **Battleground Europe** series to the Battle of Loos, which commenced on 25 September 1915. Andrew Rawson has fitted the bill admirably and his two books on the battle will make the ground far more comprehensible to the battlefield visitor.

I first visited Loos some twenty years ago, clutching Rose Coombs's invaluable *vade mecum*, **Before Endeavours Fade.** Unfortunately the industrial sprawl round about put me off exploring much further than a visit to the Memorial to the Missing at Dud Corner. A few years later I was able to spend longer on the battlefield, along with my father and under the expert guidance of one of the foremost (the foremost?) British Great War battlefield guide, Tony Spagnoly. It was only then that I began to appreciate far more fully the events that took place in the autumn of 1915 and how much of the battlefield lay on agricultural land; whilst the numerous viewpoints and vistas made understanding the action quite easy.

Loos is a tragic battle – as, of course, are all battles. But there seems to be something especially so about Loos. It was an action that certainly did not result in failure because of a lack of spirit or courage. But like all the major actions of the British army in 1915 – whether in Flanders or Gallipoli – it suffered from inexperience in all ranks and in all branches of the army. This was a consequence of the British maintaining an army that was not at all prepared for the realities of a Continental Campaign; the reasons for which go well beyond this small piece. It is facile to lay all the blame at the feet of command failings. The other element in the British failure in 1915 – and indeed for most of 1916 – was the chronic shortage of suitable artillery (and in particular heavy artillery) and reliable shells.

Loos is just about slipping from the memory of anyone alive today. The death of the Queen Mother at the end of March, 2002, perhaps marked this symbolically – her brother Fergus Bowes Lyons was killed, whist serving with the 8th Black Watch on 27 September, 1915, by an enemy bomb on the Hohenzollern Redoubt. He has no known grave and is commemorated at Dud Corner. In history books Loos is but a footnote, overwhelmed by the Shell Scandal and the squabbling between Haig and French that followed it. As a battle it is overwhelmed by the huge and lengthy struggles that took place on the Somme and around Ypres and Arras.

Loos was the testing ground for the 16th (Irish) Division when it first came to France after the battle was over. An account by Father Willie Doyle makes for graphic reading:

I stumbled across a young officer who had been badly gassed. He had got his helmet on, but was coughing and choking in a terrible way. 'For God's sake,' he cried, 'help me to tear this helmet off – I can't breathe. I'm dying.' I saw if I left him the end would not be far; so catching hold of him, I half carried, half dragged him up the trench to the aid post. I shall never forget that ten minutes; it seemed hours. I seemed to have lost all my strength: struggling with him to prevent him killing himself by tearing off his helmet made me forget almost how to breathe through mine. I was almost stifled, though safe from gas, while the perspiration simply poured from my forehead.

The aim of these books is to enable people to follow the events on the ground; but we also endeavour to bring out the personal story – like this of Father Doyle and the young officer – to ensure that we remember that war is filled with personal achievement and tragedy, and perhaps to bring more to visits to the cemeteries and memorials that scatter the battlefield today.

Nigel Cave, *Casta Natale, Rovereto, Italy*

ACKNOWLEDGEMENTS

I first came across Loos in 1989, following Rose Coombe's timeless book 'Before Endeavours Fade'. Like so many others, with Vimy Ridge and the Somme beckoning, I moved on after paying no more than a fleeting visit to the Loos Memorial at Dud Corner. Having made detailed visits to Flanders and the Somme, I was left looking for new areas to explore. A cycling tour of the villages around Bethune followed, fuelling my interest in the battle that took place there in the autumn of 1915. There was, however, a problem. Although books on later campaigns continued to appear, Loos remained a mystery. Reading the Official History, the most comprehensive account of the battle so far, convinced me that the short campaign played a key part in the history of the BEF. What followed was a five year voyage of discovery into the archives of the Battle of Loos.

Throughout my research many people have helped me learn what happened around Loos over eighty years ago. Without their assistance, my knowledge would have been far from complete. The battalion diarists, who wrote their version having witnessed the loss of many friends and comrades, deserve remembering. Under difficult circumstances they composed accurate, and often moving, accounts of the attack. This book would have not been possible without their records.

For many years Doctor John Bourne, of the University of Birmingham, has been my mentor, providing advice and encouragement along the way. Without his help, many doors would have remained unopened or unknown. Martin Middlebrook's approach to the Western Front provided the initial motivation for my visits to France and his practical advice at the beginning gave me the confidence to continue. Nigel Cave has provided assistance throughout the writing stage, answering a stream of questions with perseverance. Meanwhile, the staff at the Public Records Office in Kew tirelessly guided me through their archives. The same gratitude applies to the staff at the Imperial War Museum and without their assistance I would have failed to locate valuable information.

For the past six months Michelle Turner has worked on my hand written drafts, turning them into a presentable typescript. Meanwhile, my partner Amanda has endured endless tales of the battle. Without these people, this book would have remained an idea.

Finally, I dedicate this book to my son Alex, in the hope that his generation are never called upon to serve their country as those born a century earlier were.

ADVICE TO TOURERS

A full day can be spent studying the fighting around Loos village. The companion volume covers I Corps attack across the northern sector of the battlefield. Visitors to the Loos area have two options. If you intend to spend time on the Somme, then it is possible to stop off for a few hours, as the main route south from the channel ports passes within a few miles of the battlefield. Exit the A26 at Bully-les-Mines, taking the A21 for Lens. In about three miles leave the A21, taking the N43 sign posted for Mazingarbe and Bethune. The road dips through the Loos valley, with the huge twin slag heaps to the left and Loos village to the right. Dud Corner memorial is at the top of the rise, on the right. In order to have your car pointing in the right direction turn into the lane a few metres past the memorial, so you can turn around safely off the main road.

Alternatively if you want to explore the area in detail, you can stop near the battlefield. There are again two options. Lens has numerous hotels catering for sorts of tastes and budgets, far too numerous to list here. There are a number close to the city's railway station and all the main roads into the city eventually bring you to it. Follow signs for *centre ville* or *la gare*.

The alternative is Bethune, the home of many British soldiers for over four years. The old town was originally surrounded by ramparts, which were re-modelled by Vauban in the 18th century. It was originally a market town and the surrounding fertile plain ensured that the markets were always busy; the grain, market garden and cloth trades were particularly lucrative. When the industrial revolution arrived in the second half of the 19th century, the rich coal deposits south and east of the town ensured Bethune's place in the emerging trade markets.

In October 1914 French troops began detraining at the station during the early stages of the so-called Race to the Sea. Fierce battles to the east around La Bassée and Loos ended in a stalemate. In the spring of 1915 British troops moved into the area. During the war the town suffered heavy damage, most of which was inflicted in April 1918, when the German offensive came close to overrunning the town. Many of the inhabitants were forced to evacuate it and when they returned they found that ninety percent of the old town had been destroyed. After the war Bethune rose once again from the ruins and many of the new buildings were built to the original plans. Today it is difficult to imagine that the town was once devastated.

Bethune Belfry, focal point for many British soldiers.

The Belfry in the main square is the most striking building in the town and it was a well-known landmark for many thousands of British soldiers. The original tower was built in 1346, but it was soon replaced by a sturdier structure. An extra floor was added in 1437, and for six hundred years it has remained the town's centrepiece. A watchmen lived in the rooms at the top of the tower for many years to keep a lookout for invaders. The tower suffered a great deal of damage in 1918, and the buildings that once surrounded the base have not survived. The church on the north side of the square dates from the 16th century.

Many soldiers spent hours relaxing in streets around the square, eating, drinking or bartering for luxuries with the locals. The character of the square has been retained and on a warm summer evening, sitting outside one of the many bars, it is quite easy to imagine Tommies milling about the square in search of entertainment or mischief.

All that remained of the Belfry after the war. IWM - Q58145

A lot of the advice given below will be well known to the experienced traveller. Even so, many of you will be visiting new and unfamiliar territory. Although the battlefield is well provided with landmarks, it is easy to become lost. After all, it is possible to travel from one end of the battlefield to the other in a matter of minutes and hardly notice it.

Unlike the fighting on the Somme and in the Ypres Salient, the Battle of Loos was, for the most part, fought over open country. Trenches at this stage in the war were fairly primitive. Only later, when this area became a 'quiet sector', did both sides invest in complex trench systems. Due to the swift conclusion of the battle, there are few permanent scars such as trenches or craters, and the hard chalk provided adequate shelter from the shelling, so there are very few bunkers to see. Although Lens and Bethune lie at the heart of the French coal fields, the battlefield has suffered very few changes. The village of Loos has expanded but the layout of the streets is virtually the same as it was in 1915. Some areas on the edges of the battlefield have disappeared; some under slagheaps, others under the industrial landscape. Having said that, the area where most of the fighting took place has changed little.

11

Although there are plenty of maps in the book, you may wish to purchase the relevant IGN Series Blue map (1:25,000). 2405 est - (Lens) covers the whole battlefield, it might also be useful to also have 2405 ouest (Bethune) which covers the rear areas and Bethune town. The maps are similar to the 1:20,000 British trench maps and are very useful for detailed studies. There are 1:250000 Michelin maps available from the CWGC headquarters at Maidenhead. The maps are overprinted with the location of every Commonwealth War Graves Commission cemetery. They also include a useful index and cost about £3. Although there are a number of trench map extracts within the book showing the situation before and after the battle, you may wish to purchase the relevant sheet for the battle. The easiest way to obtain it is by joining the Western Front Association. The association runs a trench map service, the appropriate reference is 36cNW3 Loos.

The shops in and around the square in Loos provide most of what you will need. A small supermarket stocks many items, and a small bakery around the corner bakes baguettes twice a day. There are a number of bars around the square where you can quench your thirst and rest your aching feet. If you need any pills or potions for headaches or plasters for blisters, the village chemist with its Green Cross sign is just off the square. Although the village is well stocked, be warned; the shops close for lunch, although at an hour and a half long it is more like a siesta. Make sure you buy your lunch early, before 12.30, otherwise you will go hungry. On a couple of afternoons a week the village closes completely for the entire afternoon. The only other option is to return to Bethune or head into the centre of Lens.

The countryside around the village is gently undulating and walking is nearly always easy going. There are a number of suggested walks which are fairly short, so you are never very far from your car. Stout walking boots and waterproofs (in case the weather turns against you) should be all you need to get you around. It would be advisable to carry a basic first aid kit in case of accidents (it is a legal requirement to carry one in your vehicle). Although there are facilities always close to hand, it would be wise to take a supply of bottled water to quench your thirst. A few bars of chocolate never seem to go amiss either. Other useful items include a compass, binoculars and a camera. A notebook is helpful for recording your photographs; scenic views of fields can look very similar a couple of weeks later when you get them developed.

There are numerous tarmac and dirt tracks criss-crossing the battlefield, many used by the farmers to access their fields. However, in many places finding a space to park your vehicle in a safe place can be a challenge. It may seem as though the fields are deserted, but the tracks are there primarily for the farmers. Please do not leave your vehicle in such a way as to stop a tractor passing. If you wish to stop and take in a particular view, do not travel far and be ready to move along if a farmer wishes to pass. Be warned that many of these tracks have drainage ditches on each side which are often hidden by grass. Unless you are prepared to reverse long distances, keep to the main roads. Many of these trails start as tarmac lanes, but after a while turn into rough tracks that would test most cars. When it comes to wandering off the tracks, remember that the land is private. Many farmers would not object if the harvest has been gathered in, but if in doubt ask permission. Never enter a field that has crops, if you are in difficulty keep to the rough strip of ground at the edge. Remember that in this area the locals are not used to British visitors wandering about, so be prepared for a long explanation in French. There are a couple of woods on the battlefield, and the best advice is to stay out. Several areas belong to the mining companies, or one of the other local industries, and again keep out. It is possible to view virtually every part of the battlefield from many angles, so there should be no need to trespass. Remember that any sign marked 'Privée' means private land.

As for looking for relics, it is illegal to use a metal detector on someone else's property.

Above all do not set about digging. Apart from the usual dangers of tetanus, there is still a lot of ordnance buried just below the surface. In many cases shell cases litter the sides of the tracks. Artillery shells were designed to maim and kill, and some of them still can even after eighty-five years.

Artillery shells still litter the battlefield.

Relevant sources

Both the Imperial War Museum and the National Army Museum are worth a visit before you cross the Channel. They are full of interesting displays and exhibits and the IWM, in particular, possesses a useful bookshop. The IWM's reading room has a comprehensive collection of regimental and battalion histories. An appointment, either by telephone or letter, is all that is needed, although it does help if you give some indication of what you wish to view. A Reader's Ticket is needed for the NAM so take suitable ID to obtain one.

The Public Record Office is custodian to the army's war diaries, and it is well worth visiting Kew at some stage, just for the experience. Although the place appears quite daunting, the staff are very obliging, helping you in your quest for information, If you wish to pursue an individual's army career, there is a chance that their papers are stored at Kew, providing they were not destroyed in the blitz. The PRO's own publication *Army Service Records of the First World War* is a useful guide to the records held. Again take suitable ID to obtain a reader's ticket. The PRO has a website where you can look for war diary references, a great time saving device if your time in London is limited (*search for pro*).

If you intend to trace a relative who was killed, the Commonwealth War Graves Commission is usually able to help. It is usually insufficient to give just a name, because of the dozens of possibilities that will be recorded. Army details, such as regiment, battalion, rank, army number and approximate date of death help narrow down the candidates. There may be a charge according to the circumstances of the enquiry. The CWGC also has a website (search for *cwgc*), with the full Debt of Honour Register. It is well worth investigating; alternatively find a computer literate friend who can steer you through the internet. The CWGC area office is situated at Beaurains, on the southern outskirts of Arras. They also have a full listing of casualties. The care taken by the CWGC in keeping the memorials and cemeteries in pristine condition is nothing short of magnificent. Take time to record your comments in the Visitors' Books that are kept at the larger cemeteries, they are appreciated particularly in areas where there are not so many visitors.

A little planning is needed before taking your vehicle across the Channel. You need registration and insurance documents; although the Green Card system appears to have lapsed, it is worth checking first with your insurance company. A warning triangle, spare light bulbs, a first aid kit and headlight deflectors are also compulsory. Always have your passport and driving license handy in case the police perform a spot check. Although the wine is cheap and a perfect companion to a wayside picnic, be warned that the drink driving laws are stricter than in the UK. So, drivers, save the *vin rouge* for the end of the day.

It is recommended that you and your passengers have full medical and health insurance. The E111 form, available from main post offices, provides reciprocal cover. It does not, however, cover every eventuality and you may find yourself with a large bill.

Hotels

Accommodation can usually be found without difficulty in Bethune. However, there is a carnival on the weekend nearest 3 September, Liberation Day in 1944, and many hotels are booked up well in advance. The following is a sample list and some may close, while new ones open over the course of time. The Tourist information office (Tel +33 321 57 25 47), situated in the Grand Place on the ground floor of the Belfry, will be able to provide an up to date list:

> *Hotel du Vieux Beffroi, Grand Place, Bethune*
> Tel +33 321 68 15 00
> *Hotel de la Coupole, Grand Place, Bethune*
> Tel +33 321 57 35 01
> *Hotel Bernard, Place de la Gare, Bethune*
> Tel +33 321 57 20 02
> *Tour Hotel du Golf, RN43, (Rond-point St-Pry), Bethune*
> Tel +33 321 56 90 00

There are also a number of hotels in the outlying suburbs; Fouquereuil and Fonquieres to the south and Beuvy to the east.

Many hotels have restaurants, if not the town is overflowing with cafes and restaurants. Take a wander and find one that appeals to your palate and your pocket.

Useful addresses:

The Imperial War Museum, Lamberth, London SE1 6H2
Tel 020 7416 5000
The National Army Museum, Royal Hospital Road, Chelsea, London SW3 4HT
Tel 020 7730 07 17
The Commonwealth War Graves Commission, 2 Marlow Road, Maidenhead, Berks.
Tel 01628 634221
The Western Front Association, PO Box 1914, Reading, Berks.
This is the address for membership enquiries. Include a large (A4) stamped addressed envelope.

HOW TO USE THIS BOOK

If you have never visited this part of France I recommend you to take the time to read through this book (and any from the further reading section you can obtain). It is important to gain a feel for the events that took place around Loos in September 1915. This book does not intend to be a comprehensive account of the battle, even though one is long overdue. There is only a brief description of the events leading up to the battle and its aftermath. It will, however, give you a feel for the events that took place on IV Corps front.

By far the best way to appreciate the battlefield is on foot. Although the road network makes it difficult to make long walks without resorting to using roads, there are plenty of opportunities. The easiest way to tour the area is to travel from point to point by car, then take a short stroll along the tracks and paths. Walking gives you the time to study the terrain and get a feel for the lie of the land. It is impossible to take in everything while trying to concentrate at the wheel. Alternatively, you may wish to tour the whole area on a bike. Although this method of transport is an excellent compromise, there are difficulties. Many of the major roads that cross the region do not have cycle paths and at times the volume of traffic, in particular heavy lorries, can be overwhelming.

At the back of the book there are recommended car and walking tours. If time permits, and you need a full day to take in the whole of IV Corps area, follow the circular car tour first. This gives you the opportunity to see the whole area from several angles in a short space of time. You will also be able to get your bearings and identify landmarks that will help you later on. Having seen the whole area you can pick the walks that interest you according to the amount of time you have available. There is a separate section covering the cemeteries and memorials relevant to the battle.

This book is a guide to the area surrounding Loos village where thousands of men fought and died during the brief yet bloody engagement. As you walk along the paths and tracks consider the horrors and difficulties faced by the young men who came here to fight in the autumn of 1915. For the majority it was their first (and in many cases last) time in action, some had never heard a shot fired in anger before they came to Loos. On a warm dry day it is almost impossible to imagine what they faced. If this book stimulates your interest in this forgotten battle, it will have served its purpose, for the men of Loos deserve to be remembered in the same way as are their comrades of Ypres and the Somme.

Chapter One

PLANNING THE OFFENSIVE

The Battle of Loos was not an isolated assault, it was in fact one of three attacks designed to drive the Germans out of France. Preparations for an autumn offensive were well under way even before the Second Battle of Artois had drawn to a close. General Joffre

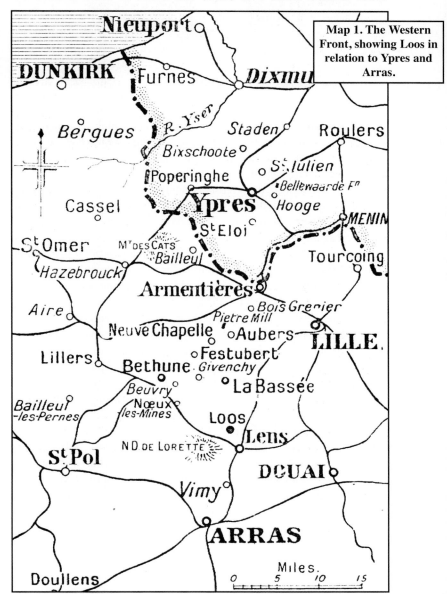

Map 1. The Western Front, showing Loos in relation to Ypres and Arras.

Field Marshal Sir John French.   **General Joffre.**   **General Sir Douglas Haig.**

proposed to throw the entire weight of his reserves against two points in the German line. It was an optimistic plan which, if successful, would push the invaders from French soil. In the Champagne region an attack driving northwards would advance towards the Ardennes. Meanwhile, a renewal of the offensive in the Artois Region would hopefully de-stabilise the Germans south of Lens. The convergent advances would then threaten the flanks of the pronounced salient astride the River Somme and River Aisne, forcing the Germans to retire across the Belgian border.

At the beginning of June General Joffre put a two-point suggestion to Field Marshal Sir John French. In order to build up an army for the Champagne offensive the British would take over the Somme region. He also wanted the British to attack alongside the French, striking the German line north of Lens. At first the proposal was accepted and First Army's commander, General Haig, was asked to prepare a plan for such an attack. A few days later Haig replied that in his opinion the Loos front was not suitable for offensive operations. The area consisted of open fields dotted with fortified villages and would be ideal defensive terrain. Instead General Haig advised that the British should strike north of the canal, as they had done in the spring.

Towards the end of June the respective general staffs and representatives from the munitions industry were in conference at Boulogne discussing plans for the following year. Their conclusions did not agree with General Joffre's plans for an autumn offensive. The spring campaign had proved that attacks on a narrow frontage could easily be contained by a small number of troops. What was needed was a broad front, up to fifteen miles wide, to enable a break though to succeed. The British would not have sufficient numbers to contribute to such an offensive until the following spring. It was also noted that only the shells of heavy calibre guns were capable of preparing the ground for the infantry, and neither army had sufficient numbers for a wide front. The spring offensives had also proved that the need for shells, in particular heavy calibre ammunition, far outstripped the current capacity of the combined munitions industries.

Although the Boulogne conference advised waiting until the following spring before taking the offensive, General Joffre was adamant that the Germans must be driven from French soil at the first opportunity. At the St Omer conference on 11 July he proposed taking the offensive at the end of August, by which time the British would have taken over the Somme front. General Joffre wanted assurances that the British would strike a simultaneous blow. However, Field Marshal French was this time more reserved in what he would offer. If the French Army broke through to the south of Lens, his Army would strike the weakened German line north of the city.

With the situation stalemated, Joffre waited until the end of July when he again asked for full co-operation from his ally at the Frevént conference. His efforts were in vain, neither general would change their views and for the next three weeks the two exchanged letters. Eventually, General Joffre, determined to press on with his plans, decided to adopt a different approach: diplomacy. On 16 August he welcomed Lord Kitchener to his headquarters for a discussion. Although there is no record of the meeting, when Kitchener visited Field Marshal French three days later it was obvious that a 'deal' had been struck. In the belief that the United Kingdom was the junior partner, he had agreed to support Joffre's plans. The following year, with the BEF swelled by the New Armies, the British would be able to argue its case on more equal terms.

There is no doubt that Kitchener would have been influenced by the global situation, for the Allies had suffered a string of set-backs throughout the summer. The attempt to knock Turkey out of the war, by invading the Dardenelles peninsula, had resulted in deadlock. Italy's first attempt to strike at the Austro-Hugarian Empire had also failed miserably. Meanwhile, in the east, the Central Powers had launched the Brest-Litovsk offensive, driving the Russians back in disarray. Kitchener was well aware that offensive action was needed on the Western Front to provide support and encouragement to their eastern ally. Lord Kitchener instructed Field Marshal French to co-operate fully with General Joffre, ordering him 'to take the offensive and act

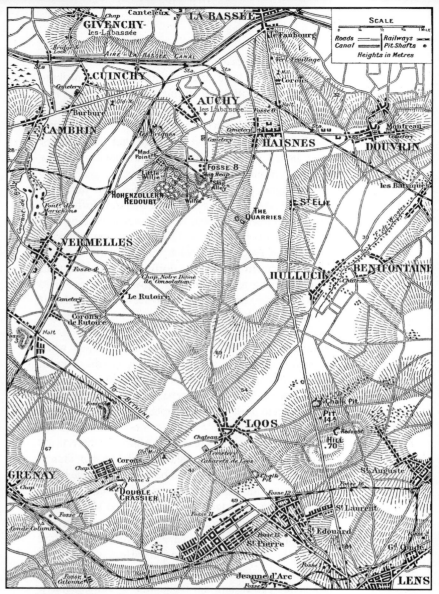

Map 2. Schematic map of First Army's battlefield.

vigorously'. To make up for the shortfall in artillery, gas would be used to surprise the Germans. As August drew to a close, plans were being drawn up and before long men and equipment began flooding into the Bethune area.

GHQ neither wanted the attack, nor was it on their chosen ground. However, to prove to the Germans that the Allies were united, the

British Army had to act. In Kitchener's own words;

> *...we must act with all energy and do our utmost to help France in their offensive, even though by doing so we may suffer heavy losses*

The date was originally set for 8 September, but delays in preparing the Champagne sector for action forced a postponement until the 25th.

There were two plans. If the weather allowed the use of gas, General Haig's First Army would attack between the La Bassée canal and Lens with six divisions of I and IV Corps. A third corps, IX, was in reserve alongside the cavalry. Meanwhile, First Army's remaining two corps, the Indian and III Corps, would make subsidiary attacks north of the canal. General Plumer's Second Army would also carry out a number of diversionary attacks in Flanders, designed to deceive the Germans and pin down their reserves. However, if gas could not be deployed, the attack on First Army's front would be scaled down considerably. On IV Corps front, 15th (Scottish) Division would attack the German line west of Loos, seizing Loos Road and Lens Road redoubts. Meanwhile, the 9th (Scottish) Division, on I Corps front, would capture Hohenzollern Redoubt and Fosse 8. Further attacks would follow when the weather allowed the gas to be used. The offensive would be called off if the wind remained unfavourable on the 26th and 27th.

Meanwhile, Joffre was fully occupied finalising his own plan. The French Army would attack at two points, the first of which was only a few miles south of the British attack. Tenth Army, with seventeen divisions, would attack on a twelve mile front supported by over 400 heavy calibre guns (the British had seventy). General d'Urbal was to advance from Vimy Ridge, driving east of Lens to link up with General Haig's men. The British and French would then continue to push east across the Douai plain. The attack in the Champagne would strike the German positions east of Reims. Second Army, employing twenty-seven infantry and six cavalry divisions, would attack on an eighteen mile front supported by 850 heavy guns. Meanwhile, Fourth Army would carry out a subsidiary attack west of Reims. It was hoped that General Pétain would be able to push north towards the Ardennes. The main objective was the railway line linking Meziéres and Hirson, an advance of forty miles! If successful the German Army would be split in two, allowing the cavalry to rush forward to the Belgian border.

As darkness fell across France on the evening of 24 September 1915, thousands of men took up their positions ready for zero hour. It was the British army's largest battle of the war so far, and the first in which Kitchener's New Army divisions were involved.

Chapter Two

THE BATTLEFIELD IN 1915

The front held by Lieutenant-General Henry Rawlinson's IV Corps ran approximately north to south, crossing the Lens - Bethune road to the west of Loos. Using three divisions, the attack would develop eastwards, with the right hand division holding a refused flank. Lieutenant-General Hubert Gough's I Corps would advance on Rawlinson's left. What follows is a description of the ground covered by each division, combined with an outline of First Army's plan. Each part starts in the division's rear area, working east across No Man's

Map 3. A detailed map of IV Corps area showing the German lines of defence.

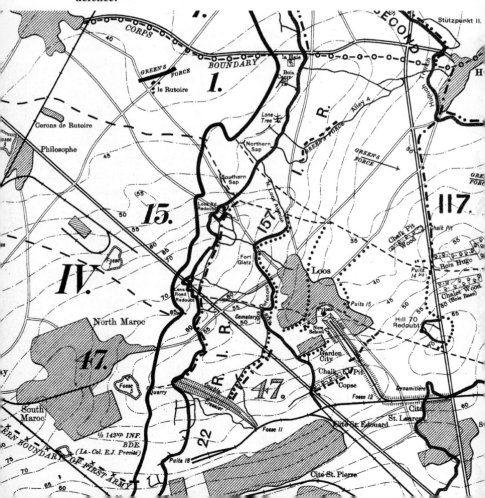

Land as far as the high water mark of the British advance, in many cases close to the German second line of defence.

The left-hand boundary of IV Corps ran along the road between Vermelles, which lay behind the British front, and Hulluch, behind the German line. Major-General Holland's 1st Division occupied the sector immediately south of the road. Vermelles, a large and thriving village, provided shelter for a variety of support services. The imposing chateau, at the southern end of the village, was used by a number of advanced dressing stations during the war. Another ADS occupied the cellars of the village brewery, although during the battle casualties were taken elsewhere. Throughout the battle the village played host to a number of divisional headquarters, and its streets would have been filled with troops moving to and from the front. Two of the tallest structures in the village, the church and the water tower, provided observation platforms for artillery spotters.

The ground between Vermelles and No Man's Land was flat, open and barren. The only cluster of

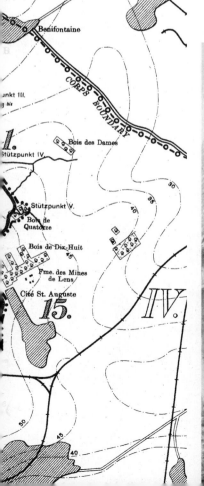

British observation officer and sniper overlooking German trenches.

buildings in the middle of the fields was, and still is, Le Rutoire Farm, which stood to the rear of 1st Division's sector. Before the battle No Man's Land was nearly half a mile wide, neither side wishing to antagonise the other by claiming territory. All this changed in September 1915. Several lines of trenches were excavated in No Man's Land to accommodate the assault troops, whilst an extra trench to hold the hundreds of gas cylinders was also dug. This operation narrowed No Man's Land considerably but, even so, General Holland's men would have to cross 400 metres of open ground to reach the Germans. Before the war the land had been farmed, but twelve month of neglect had reduced it to an unkempt scrub. In many places the wild crops screened the barbed wire and trenches, making accurate registration impossible.

There were small two copses in No Man's Land on the left of the division's front, la Haie and Bois Carré. Although the shelling had reduced the trees to smashed stumps, each one concealed a German observation post, linked by saps to the front line. A few hundred metres to the south, again in No Man's Land, stood a large cherry tree, marked on the British trench maps as Lone Tree. The shattered trunk managed to produce blossom in the spring of 1915 in spite of the shrapnel and bullets that became embedded in it.

The trench lines ran north to south on the western slopes of what is known as the Grenay Ridge, although in this sector the slope is barely noticeable. Even so, in flat country the slightest advantage in height makes observation far easier. In places slight undulations hid the German front line and its protective belt of barbed wire. As was usually the case, the Germans held the high ground and their front line ran

along the forward slope. The support line had been dug along the crest of the ridge, affording excellent views across the British rear.

Moving east into the German rear area, the ground drops gently towards Hulluch. A support trench, known as Gun Trench, ran along the reverse slope and a number of communications trenches criss-crossed the area. At the foot of the incline the main highway connecting Lens and La Bassée runs in a straight line north to south across the battlefield. In 1915 a line of poplar trees ran alongside the road. Hulluch village is just to the east of the road and it faced the left sector of 1st Division. A Chalk Pit and its adjacent wood stood close to the Lens road on the right of the division's front. Just beyond, alongside the road, was Puits 14 bis, a small mine head complex; the pithead chimney was an important landmark for many soldiers. Bois Hugo, a thin strip of woodland, ran eastwards from the mine, marking the boundary between the 1st and 15th Division.

The German Second Line would play an important role during the battle, in particular the section between Hulluch and Bois Hugo. The trench ran around the outskirts of the village coming from the north. It then turned at right angles, heading east across the open moor. It again turned a right angle and ran south, 400 metres east of the Lens – La Bassée road. It was positioned to cover the valley north of Loos, and could fire on troops as soon as they crossed the summit of Grenay Ridge. Two strong points, know as Stutzpunkz III and IV, anchored the line.

View from the crest of the Grenay Ridge. The distant line of trees stand alongside the Lens - La Bassée road; the German Second Line crossed the fields beyond. IWM - Q43120

Crude trenches wound their way around the mining communities east of Bethune.

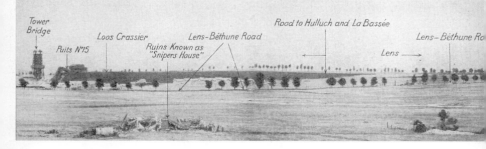

Tower Bridge

Puits Nº15

Loos Crassier

Ruins Known as "Snipers House"

Lens-Béthune Road

Road to Hulluch and La Bassée

Lens →

Lens-Béthune Ro

The ground held by the 15th (Scottish) Division was similar to 1st Division's sector. A number of small mining communities, primarily Philosophe and Mazingarbe, housed the headquarters and field ambulances. The Scots held a line of trenches along the lower slopes of the Grenay ridge, which in this sector is more noticeable. Again the Germans held the crest of the ridge, with their fire trench on the forward slope. At two points the front line had been fortified with strong emplacements, Loos Road Redoubt and Lens Road Redoubt. Both were designed to conduct an all round defence, capable of holding out if the line either side fell into British hands. Just beyond the support line,

Loos pithead, nicknamed Tower Bridge, was a familiar landmark on the battlefield.

the ground falls rapidly to the outskirts of Loos. A defensive line followed the western outskirts of the village.

The village of Loos had grown around Puits Number 15, and was a thriving community before the war. The twin pithead towers, known as 'Tower Bridge' by many, could be seen for miles around. A huge wall of slag, nick-named the 'Grandstand', stretched east from the towers, and a railway ran along the summit connecting the mine to the rest of the network. The ground rises rapidly to the east of the village, culminating in a flat summit known as Hill 70. It was possible to see for miles from the hill, and the Germans had built a semi-circular redoubt to protect the natural observation platform. The Lens - La Bassée road crosses the top of the hill and continues south into the Lens suburbs. In 1915 the area east and south of the hill was in the early stages of development. Two mining villages, Cité St Auguste to the west and Cité St Laurent to the south, had been incorporated into

Panorama of the German held territory south of Loos.

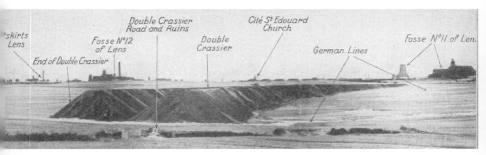

the German secondary line. This trench had been built out of artillery range, and it had been placed to stop any further advance if Hill 70 fell.

The southern flank of IV Corps was held by the 47th (London) Division. For once the Germans did not hold the high ground and from the left of the Division's front it was possible to see the whole of the Loos valley. Heading east, the ground fell rapidly, and the Lens highway cut across the valley at an angle. The Londoners would have to capture the southern outskirts of Loos village; the village defence line curved in an arc around the edge of the houses. At one point it ran along the edge of the village cemetery, and the Germans made use of the crypts to shelter from the shelling. The defence line then swung east past a small housing estate, built in the market garden style. The Londoners named the isolated estate Welwyn Garden City. The ground rises quickly to the south of Loos, and in 1915 a thin strip of woodland, known as Chalk Pit Wood, stretched across the slope north of the Lens road.

The front line on the centre of 47th Division's front sloped down to the floor of the Loos valley. An intermediate trench ran across the valley floor, connected at its north end to the Loos defence line. Mining activity had left a great scar across the valley, the slag heap known as Double Crassier. In 1915 the mounds of ash formed two long strips, running east to west behind the German line. Light railways, which carried coal-trucks filled with slag, ran along the crests of the two mounds. Double Crassier was about fifteen metres high and from its summit it was possible to dominate any advance across the Loos valley. Puits No 11 stood at the eastern end of the Crassier, on the horizon. Around the foot of the mine was the community of Cité St Edouard.

The right hand brigade of the London Division did not attack on the morning of the 25th. The troops holding this part of the line faked an attack to deceive the Germans. These 'attacks' were commonplace later in the war and known as 'Chinese Attacks'.

Chapter Three

THE MEN

First Army's plan called for two corps to attack side by side south of the La Bassée Canal. Lieutenant-General Gough's I Corps held the left, or northern, half of the front with three divisions. 2nd Division, on the left of the front, would advance astride the canal and form a protective flank to the east of Auchy-lez-la-Bassée. Meanwhile, the 9th (Scottish) Division and the 7th Division would advance east through Haisnes and Hulluch. Lieutenant-General Rawlinson's IV Corps also had three divisions to accomplish its task. 1st Division, on the left of the front, would advance alongside I Corps past Hulluch. The 15th (Scottish) Division, in the centre of the corps, would capture Loos village before making its way towards Cité St Auguste. The southern flank would be secured by the 47th (London) Division, in touch with the Tenth French Army.

First Army also had a substantial reserve in place, three divisions of IX Corps and a single cavalry division. 21st Division was billeted in and around Beuvry, five miles behind I Corps front, while 24th Division camped near Nouex-les-Mines, six miles behind IV Corps. The two would take over the advance into open country. The Guards Division was stationed to the west of Bethune as the final reserve. The 3rd Cavalry Division would be ready to exploit any breakthrough. The Cavalry Corps was placed about twenty miles behind First Army's front, ready to deliver the final blow.

Lieutenant-General Sir Henry Rawlinson Bt.

IV Corps divisions were all different in nature, having come from a variety of backgrounds. Some were veterans of several campaigns, while others would be going into battle for the first time. Many wanted to see how the New Army divisions fared against the Germans. What follows is a brief background of each division to illustrate the differences.

LOOS
25TH SEPT, 1915.
DISPOSITIONS AT ZERO, 6.30 A.M.

N

19. 58th

**INDIAN
CORPS**

Chaplle St Roch

Roch Alley

Canteleux

LA BASSÉE

I Bⁿ/56 I.R.

II Bⁿ/16 I.R.

Corps Boundary

Givenchy 54th

Canal

2.

Towpath Alley

Canal Alley

I Bⁿ/16 I.R.

Cuinchy 54th

Auchy lez la Bassée

14.

II/JÄGER

Haisnes

Douvrin

Douvrin 2½

Wingles 1 Mile

mbrin

194th

Les Briqu

Petin Alley

Stpkt. I.

II d

27th

28th

9. 26th

Corons

The Dump
Hohenzollern
Redoubt

I COY.
II R.I.R.

I COY, II R.R.R.

Quarries

Cité St Elie

Green Alley South

Stpkt. II.

I Bⁿ/II R.I.R.
(at Wingles)

mnelles

7.

22nd

20th

Corps Boundary

Hulluch

SECOND LINE

Benifontaine

Pont à Vendin
2½ Miles

I Bⁿ/157 I.R.

I Bⁿ/157 I.
(at Pont à Ve

1.

GREEN'S FORCE

le Rutoire

3rd

1st

Box
Carré

Lone Tree

Alley 4

2nd

Stpkt. III.

G

Béthune
8 Miles

Stpkt. IV.

15.

46th

157

Loos Rd. Redoubt

117.

I Bⁿ/157 I.R.

Bois Hugo

Stpkt. V.

Annay 1¼ Mile

Fosse 7

44th

I Bⁿ/157 I.R.

Puits 14bis

Hamlet Wood

Cité St Auguste

IV

142nd

137th

Loos Rd. Redoubt

Loos

Hill 70
Redoubt

I COY
22 R.I.R.

3 COS., 22 R
(at Vendin

renay

North Maroc

140th

Garden City

Dynamitière

Harnes 3 M

South Maroc

142nd

Double Crassier

Stpkt. 69.

I Bⁿ/22 R.I.R.

Fosse 12

Fosse 11

Cité St Edouard

Fosse Vendin
7 M

Lens 1½

XXI.

Puits 16

Cité St Pierre

LENS

Garvin
6 m.

Dosai 10 Mil

SCALE

YARDS 1000   0   1000   2000 YARDS

MILE   ½   0   ½   1

Stpkt. I,II,III,IV,V.   Stützpunkt (Redoubt) I,II,III,IV,V.

Fire Trenches.   Communication Trenches.

CORPS LIV. Divisions, 1,2, etc. Infantry Bdes. 20th, 22nd, etc.

Divisional Boundary.   Brigade Boundary.

**Map 4. First Army's dispositions at
zero hour.**

IV Corps - THE ASSUALT TROOPS

1st Division

1st Division was one of the original BEF divisions that landed in France in August 1914. It managed to avoid major engagements during the retreat from Mons. Even so, on a number of occasions, the Division was forced into fighting rear-guard actions. During the battle of the Aisne the Division suffered heavy casualties as it tried to advance onto the heights above the river. The following month the BEF moved to Flanders and in the fighting that followed 1st Division was virtually wiped out defending the Ypres Salient. After the battle the survivors moved south and spent the winter digging trenches astride the La Bassée Canal. The Division was brought up to strength with reservists, ex-soldiers who had been recalled to the colours.

On 9 May the Division participated in I Corps offensive south of Neuve Chapelle, as part of the Battle of Aubers Ridge. The attack was a complete disaster; in a matter of minutes two brigades lost over two thousand officers and men, sixty percent of their fighting strength. After the battle the Division returned to the La Bassée canal area and for a second time welcomed a new batch of reservists.

In August the Division's 1 Brigade lost its Guards status when the 1st Coldstream Guards and the 1st Scots Guards left to join the new Guards Division. Two New Army battalions, the 8th Royal Berkshires and the 10th Gloucesters, took their place. The newcomers were not welcomed, at this stage of the war regular soldiers viewed Kitchener's men with suspicion. The Division suffered a second loss at the end of the month when Major-General Haking was promoted to lead IX Corps, First Army's reserve. Major-General Arthur Holland had little time to adjust to his new command before it took over the trenches east of Vermelles.

15th (Scottish) Division

On 11 September 1914 Army Order 382 authorised the formation of a Second New Army, and within days 15th Division began to assemble at Aldershot, using the surplus personnel of the 9th (Scottish) Division. 44 Brigade was composed of Highland regiments, while 45 Brigade recruits came from the borders and 46 Brigade included two battalions from each area.

At the end of the month the Division paraded in front of the King, but in the absence of equipment, all but the staff-officers were still dressed in their own civilian clothes. As winter set in, the men moved

Scottish troops prepare for their first battle. IWM - Q60739

into billets on Salisbury Plain. Looking back, the efforts to prepare the men for war were ludicrous. They do, however, illustrate how unprepared Great Britain was for a full-scale war. On 22 January Lord Kitchener and Monsieur Millerand inspected the men, who were now proudly wearing their new uniforms. The French Minister for War was rather perturbed that only the front ranks carried arms, and they consisted of an array of obsolete rifles dating from the previous century.

The artillery suffered even greater difficulties in their attempts to train. Horses arrived at an early stage, but in the absence of harnesses and saddles the prospective riders were forced to practice on wooden dummies for several months. At first the only 'artillery-piece' available for drill purposes consisted of a funeral carriage, with a log tied on top! Eventually resourceful officers stole a muzzle loading gun from the Ordnance Officers' mess to use for exercises. The first supply of 'real' artillery pieces arrived in the spring, and they consisted of a mixture of obsolete fifteen pounders and French breach loaders. The guns that were to accompany the Division overseas eventually arrived in the summer of 1915. However, the gun-sights only turned up a few days before departure.

Nevertheless, enthusiasm and hard work made up for the lack of equipment and by the summer the troops were eager to embark for France. On 21 June the King inspected the division on Sidbury Hill,

and the formation he saw was a complete contrast to the rabble he had seen nine months earlier. A few days later orders to leave for the coast arrived and, by the middle of July, the 15th (Scottish) Division was stationed in the Bethune area. After a period of acclimatisation the men entered the trenches on the Grenay Ridge opposite Loos.

47th (London) Division

The 47th (London) Division, a Territorial formation, was recruited in the south-west and south-east districts of the capital. When war broke out the infantry were encamped on Salisbury Plain, engaged in their annual manoeuvres. The troops were immediately recalled and sent to the St Albans area, to guard roads and installations. Training continued, and in October Major-General Sir Charles Barter was informed that his Division had been selected for overseas duties.

Orders to cross the Channel eventually arrived on 2 March 1915 and by the end of the month the Londoners were billeted in the villages

London Territorials in training.

around Bethune. Before long the Division was holding the front line astride the La Bassée Canal, including Festubert, Givenchy and Cuinchy. Although the divisional artillery provided supporting fire for the attack on Aubers Ridge on 9 May, the infantry took no part in the engagement. Elements did take part in the attacks on Festubert a week later, but for many the attack south of Loos would be their first battle. At the end of June the French army handed over the line west of Loos to First Army and throughout the summer Barter's Division held sectors on the Grenay Ridge. After a short break, 47th Division took over the Maroc sector on the southern flank of the BEF. Over the next three weeks the men were kept busy, digging over three miles of trenches in preparation for the forthcoming battle.

IX CORPS - THE RESERVES

21st and 24th Divisions - formation and training

On 13 September Army Order No. 388 authorised the formation of a Third New Army, in response to the overwhelming influx of volunteers. Throughout the month six divisions, numbered 21st to 26th, began to assemble on Salisbury Plain, their ranks quickly filled by the overflow of recruits from the Second New Army. Two of these divisions would endure their baptism of fire on the Loos battlefield. 21st Division recruited in the north east of England and the three brigades were comprised of Yorkshire and Northumberland regiments. 24th Division's volunteers came from a variety of towns across the south and east of England.

By the end of September the pool of experienced officers had almost dried up. Instructors were hard to come by, virtually all the retired officers had joined up, and officers recovering from wounds were quickly posted overseas to the regular army. At most a battalion had only one or two officers with any previous experience. Bankers, clerks and students became officers; teachers and policemen were promoted to sergeant and corporal. In many cases a man received his stripes because of his well-dressed appearance. Even so, the recruits took to their new ranks with enthusiasm. The 21st soon moved from its billets at Tring to encampments at Halton Park, while the 24th left for Shoreham. Without weapons or uniforms, training options were limited, but days were filled with drills, parades and marches. Country lanes were filled with columns of men, dressed in a hotchpotch of clothes and boots, much to the amusement of the locals. Winter weather forced the men under cover and churches, cinemas and halls were filled to the brim with shabbily dressed men. The first batch of uniforms arrived in spring; not khaki as expected, but a selection of civilian outfits including a batch of red and blue Post-Office uniforms. Equipment, much of it obsolete or of foreign origin, also began to appear. As time passed, Kitchener's men began to look like soldiers and, with plans for new offensives in the pipeline, the War Office and GHQ started to take them seriously.

As spring turned to summer, the divisions assembled on Salisbury Plain where the men were allowed to practice musketry. At the end of August, following inspections by Field Marshal Kitchener and the King, embarkation orders arrived and men said their last farewells before leaving for France. 24th Division completed its assembly near Etaples on 4 September, while 21st Division reached its billets near St Omer nine days later. There was, however, little time to enjoy the delights of the new surroundings.

On 18 September orders arrived instructing the two divisions to move south to Bethune, where they would come under IX Corps, First Army's reserve. For three nights in a row the men marched along the country lanes, sometimes covering over twenty miles. Many were pushed to the limit by the hot weather and long marches. Yet by the evening of the 23rd they had reached Lillers, to the west of Bethune.

Another endless route march.

As darkness fell on the 24th the two divisions again moved, this time forward towards the sounds of battle. 21st Division gathered to the east of Bethune near Beuvry, while 24th Division assembled south of the town near Noeux-les-Mines, both were five or six miles behind the front line. It was a difficult night for many and in some areas lack of experience among the transport drivers caused interminable delays. Some units took more than eight hours to travel six or seven miles. Lieutenant-General Haking, IX Corps' commanding officer, summed up the problems:

I am of the opinion that the delay was caused chiefly by their own indifferent march discipline, especially as regards first-line transport. These divisions only received their transport just before leaving England, their drivers were not well trained and the march discipline of these new divisions, though good when marching without transport, was certainly not good when marching with it, and constant halts and checks occurred.

The Guards Division

The formation of the Guards Division was, and still is, a controversial issue. In the summer of 1915 Lord Kitchener proposed the idea of forming an élite division in the British Expeditionary Force, in the hope it would set a standard for others to aspire. Some camps opposed the suggestion on the grounds that it was unwise to concentrate the Guards battalions into one formation. As usual Kitchener persisted, and in July the King approved the proposal. A few weeks later Major-General the Earl of Cavan established his headquarters at Lumbres, near St Omer, and began welcolming his new battalions.

Contrary to common believe, the Guards were not all battle-hardened regulars. Three of the infantry battalion came direct from England, having been built from scratch by emptying the depots of personnel. The divisional artillery was composed of New Army men who were in the process of being trained. The three field artillery brigades were taken from the 16th (Irish) Division. The howitzer brigade came from the 11th (Northern) Division; the brigade had been left behind when the Division left for Gallipoli at the end of June, bound for Suvla Bay. After a short period of training the Division moved south, arriving in the Bethune area on 24 September. It was intended that the Guards would spearhead the break out into open country.

First Army also had the 3rd Cavalry Division allotted to it. As usual, the cavalry troopers were never used as intended and briefly held the trenches in and around Loos.

36

THE GERMANS

All too often we ignore the Germans who faced British attacks. Yet it was often their tenacity and resilience that thwarted Allied offensives, even in the face of overwhelming numbers, horrific bombardments and, at Loos, gas. In the spring of 1915 the German Army underwent the first of several reorganisations. Many of the Western Front divisions donated one of their four regiments to form a new series of divisions (101st to 123rd, odd numbers only). The 117th Division, facing IV Corps, was formed in April, near Liart in Seventh Army's area, from this pool of regiments.

Two of the regiments, the 11th Reserve and 12th Reserve, had participated in the VI Reserve Corps advance to the Meuse under Fifth Army. Following a number of costly engagements in September 1914 to the north-west of Verdun they took up positions on the hills west of the town. They remained here on the defensive until the 117th Division was formed. The third regiment, the 157th, also served under the Crown Prince's Fifth Army during the advance to the Marne. It advanced as far south as Layencourt, over thirty miles south-west of Verdun, before retiring back to the Champagne. It eventually took up positions to the east of Rheims, holding them until recalled to Liart.

Soon after the 117th Division formed it was transferred to the Artois in response to French attacks south of Arras. Almost immediately the division was called upon to hold the line, and throughout May and June it fought costly engagements near Souchez and on the infamous Notre Dame Lorrete. Following these battles, in which the 117th suffered nearly 5,500 casualties, the Division moved to Lille to refit. In July it took over the Loos sector, spending the next two months improving the trenches and constructing a new line of defence 2,000 metres behind the front.

On 25 September the Division had two regiments, or six battalions, facing IV Corps front. The 157th Regiment held the front line opposite the 1st and 15th Divisions with a single battalion. Two companies, about 400 men, faced each division. The support battalion was stationed about half a mile behind the front, many of its men in Loos itself. The reserve battalion was in billets four or five miles in the rear, about three hours march away from the front line. In case of attack it would be expected to man the second line of defence between Hulluch and Cité St Auguste. The 22nd Reserve Battalion held the line opposite the 47th (London) Division. However, only the two northern companies would be attacked. The rest of the Battalion faced a fake, or 'Chinese', attack planned to prevent reserves attacking IV Corps right flank. The support and reserve battalions were billeted in the outskirts of Lens. The 117th's third regiment was in line opposite I Corps and played no direct part in IV Corps attack. Apart from local reserves the Crown Prince of Bavaria's Sixth Army could call upon two divisions, although only the 8th Division eventually faced IV Corps. It was, however, many miles in the rear, refitting near Tourcoing and Roubaix, when the attack began.

The German Defences

For twelve months the Loos front had been quiet, while the Allies attacked the German line to the north and to the south. Until the spring of 1915 the Germans had relied on a single system of trenches to hold the Grenay Ridge; only in front of Loos had they dug an intermediate line to protect the village. Following the Allied spring offensives it became obvious that a single line could easily be broken, leaving the rear area vulnerable. Faced with waging a defensive war in the West, while employing the minimum number of troops, the German tacticians decided to supplement the front with a second line of defence. This line would be built, without interference, over a mile behind the front, far beyond the reach of Allied guns. Where it was possible, villages and woods would be incorporated into the line.

Meanwhile the Germans made every effort to make their front line positions as strong and as comfortable as possible. Strong wide belts of wire stretched in front of the trenches, while saps strategically placed in No Man's Land made sure that the garrison would not be taken by surprise. Chalk just beneath the surface made it possible to dig deep dugouts to protect the men from shellfire.

Two after-the-battle reports give an interesting insight into how well the Germans had prepared themselves on the Grenay Ridge. The first, which was submitted by the 2nd King's Royal Rifle Corps, is a detailed study of the line opposite 2 Brigade near Lone Tree. As the same German battalion manned the whole sector opposite 1st Division, there is no reason to doubt that it was representative of the positions facing the IV Corps left.

Cut deep into the chalk, the German trenches provided protection from everything but a direct hit.

They seemed to be a bluff and not nearly so strong as shown by air photo. The wire in front of us was about 10ft wide, very low and thick barbed wire. The saps to which we had paid great attention were hardly a foot deep.

Artillery officers were anxious to discover if their bombardment had managed to damage the German defences. However, in 2 Brigade's sector, as in many other areas, they were to be disappointed. Four days of shelling had failed to make a serious impact on the trenches:

The front line trench was in perfect condition and hardly touched. Communication trenches deep and narrow. Trenching very well kept and clean. Lockers for everything including 'GAS SHUTE', rifle racks etc. Trench rather wide with fire step. Front revetted and staked up, assisted by wire netting. Telephone wires found but no 'phone. Equipment new – rifles marked 1915. Bottom of trench was boarded out with drain underneath.

The munitions prediction of the need for more heavy calibre guns and ammunition had proved to be true. Apart from more guns and ammunition, new methods of observation and registration would be required. Altogether the German trenches were a permanent, well-maintained system of defence made by an opponent intent on a long occupation. They were somewhat different to the hastily dug assembly

39

used by the British troops a few hundred yards away. They were cramped, muddy and in the wet autumn weather served as perfect drainage channel.

The KRRC also discovered a surprising substitute for barbed wire beyond the front line, visible only from the air.

The wire along the communications trenches was a bluff. Thistles being planted in rows which at a short distance looked like strong wire.

Further south on 15th Division's front, the Germans had again dug deep into the chalk, making shell-proof shelters.

The Guards Division spent the night of 26 September in reserve on the Grenay Ridge and the Grenadier Guards were impressed by their temporary accommodation.

Both officers and men were filled with admiration at the intricate dug-outs they found, twenty to thirty feet down in the chalk; evidently great trouble had been expended on this part of the line, and the German officers had been accustomed to live almost in luxury.

This was the condition of the German front line after the British artillery had spent four days trying to destroy it.

GAS OPERATIONS

The German Army first used gas in a significant way on the Western Front in a surprise attack on the Ypres Salient in late April 1915. Despite widespread condemnation of this new, terrible weapon, both the War Office and the British Army recognised its potential and Lord Kitchener immediately appointed Colonel Louis Jackson RE to conduct a feasibility study. Research at the Imperial College of Science quickly identified that chlorine despatched from pressurised cylinders would be the most effective method to form a 'gas cloud'. The system of delivery worked along the same principles as a soda syphon. A tube inserted into the cylinder allowed the gas to escape under pressure, and the speed of release was controlled by a stop cock. Spraying out along a half-inch diameter iron tube, three metres long (copper tubing was preferred but it was in scarce supply), the liquid chlorine converted into a yellowish-white gas as it emerged into the atmosphere.

The first cylinders were tested at the beginning of June at Runcorn, before members of the War Office. Employees from the Castner-Keller factory took part in the experiment, standing at intervals in front of the

An early form of gas mask. The hood should be tucked into the tunic before going into action.

advancing cloud with orders to signal when it reached them. The men then timed how long they could stand the poison before pulling on a smoke helmet, a barbaric yet effective method of measurement. The gas release had to last for longer than thirty minutes, the effective life span of a German gas mask. There was, however, a problem with the scheme. Calculations showed that British industry could not produce enough chlorine to cover the whole of First Army's front. Instead it was proposed to use smoke candles to increase the life-span of the 'gas-cloud'.

The War Office were convinced and sanctioned the formation of the first gas unit under Lieutenant-Colonel Foulkes. Under a cloud of secrecy chemical students from across the country (and those already enlisted in the army) were asked to join the new formation. The volunteers knew nothing of their task until they arrived at Helfaut depot near St Omer. Everyone was given the option to leave once they had been briefed, but very few returned to England. Many came straight from civilian life and knew little of army discipline. Foulkes arranged a crash course in pistol shooting, navigation and the assessment of wind direction. A two-day tour of the front line followed, after which the chemical students were debriefed and encouraged to suggest ways in which their own training could be improved.

Meanwhile, the energetic Foulkes was kept busy collecting equipment, chasing suppliers and attending army conferences, where he was faced with a mixture of interest and cynicism. On 22 August General Haig, surrounded by his commanders, staff officers and engineers, and filled with suspicion, witnessed a mock gas attack at the Special Brigade's headquarters. It was, however, an answer to the Army's shortage of artillery.

All along the front engineers supervised the digging of a gas trench, in places up to fifty metres in front of the assault trench, complete with emplacements ready to take the cylinders. There were typically six engineer sections on each divisional front, and a section controlled about twelve gas batteries. The men were split into twos and each pair was responsible for one of the batteries, which consisted of twelve cylinders. Meanwhile, the infantry were given the unenviable task of carrying the cylinders forward. The cylinders were slung on special slings and during the nights before the battle the men struggled along the trenches cursing their heavy loads. Everyone was suspicious; although gas had been given the code name 'Accessory Number 1', most soldiers knew what their deadly cargo contained. Even so, there were no accidents and by the night of the 24th over 1,500 cylinders were in place.

General Haig was briefed on the weather situation by his meteorological officer, Captain E Gold, throughout the day. Reports from London and Paris were compared with results taken by a number of observation stations in First Army area. Every hour reports from the front line came in from Foulkes' men, completing the picture. At 9.00pm Gold informed General Haig that the Met Office forecast gave favourable conditions for the morning. On the strength of the report, the order went out to prepare to assault.

> *The weather forecast at this hour, indicates that a west or south-west wind may be anticipated tomorrow, 25th September. All orders issued for the attack with gas will therefore hold good. The hour of zero will be notified during the night.*

All along the front men moved into position, while the reserves moved closer to the action. By 2.30am Haig knew that everything was in place, and the ultimate decision rested on his shoulders. He was concerned that updated forecast showed that the wind was swinging to the south and its speed was falling close to the desired minimum. After a final briefing with Captain Gold, the time was set. The gas

Gas mask drill, checking the hoods for damage.

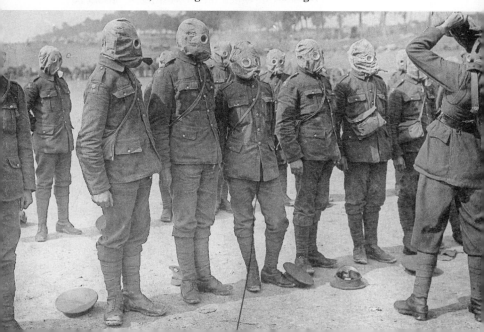

programme would began at sunrise (5.50am), the infantry would 'go over the top' forty minutes later. Lieutenant F D Charles controlled part of 15th Division's sector, and his account describes the hours before zero:

> On arrival at the trenches our first job was to put everything in order in preparation for the attack, the exact hour of which was to be telegraphed later, and each man was instructed to put on his brassard [armband], a red white and green vertically striped affair, which, if clean, could not very well be mistaken for a staff officer. It served as our authority for giving orders, and also as a preventative against being ordered 'over the top' with the assaulting infantry.
>
> The time of the attack was telegraphed to me at 4.40am. The infantry, after being told the time of the attack by us, issued a rum ration to each man who wanted it, and then started getting their men together, instructing them slowly and without hurry and very clearly, so that each man knew what to do when the time came.

While the assault troops made their last minute preparations, First Army staff waited impatiently at Hinges Chateau. Although the weather stations reported favourable conditions, the air was calm and at 5.00am Haig went outside with his senior ADC, Major A F Fletcher. At Haig's request Fletcher lit a cigarette and the two watched as the smoke drifted to the north-east. The order was given to proceed, and Haig climbed to the top of his observation platform to watch the horizon. Even at this late hour there were reservations, and at about 5.30am a staff officer was ordered to telephone I Corps to ask if the attack could be called off. It was, however, too late to alter the decision.

At 5.50am Foulkes' men went into action, following the programme below:

Minutes	
Zero Hour	Start the gas and run six cylinders one after the other at full blast until they are exhausted.
0.12 to 0.20	Start the smoke. The smoke is to run concurrently with the gas if the gas is not exhausted at 0.12.
0.20	Start the gas again and run six cylinders one after the other at full blast until they are all exhausted.
0.32 to 0.40	Start the smoke again. The smoke is to run concurrently with the gas if the gas is not exhausted at 0.32.
0.38	Turn all the gas off punctually. Thicken up smoke with triple candles.
	Prepare for assault
0.40	ASSAULT

Chapter Four

1ST DIVISION'S ASSAULT

1 Brigade

1 Brigade, under the command of Brigadier-General Anthony Reddie, was on the left of 1st Division's assault, immediately south of the Vermelles-Hulluch Road. 7th Division, the right hand division of Lieutenant-General Sir Hubert Gough, would attack on the Brigade's left flank. During August, 1 Brigade had, as previously discussed, exchanged two Guard battalions for two K3 Kitchener battalions. Despite their inexperience, Reddie had chosen to lead with his new additions. The reason for this is not documented, but it had been acknowledged that regular soldiers had developed a tendency to become pinned down in the face of heavy fire. It may be that Reddie hoped to capitalize on the enthusiasm and innocence of the New Army men to break through the first line of trenches. His experienced battalions could then push on towards Hulluch. The Brigade was deployed at zero hour with 8th Royal Berkshires on the left, the 10th Gloucesters on the right, the 1st Cameron Highlanders in support and the 1st Black Watch in reserve. A fifth battalion, the 1/14th London (London Scottish), was seconded to Colonel Green's reserve force in support behind the centre of the division.

As the gas officers started the first release the German artillery

Map 5. 1st Division's deployment south of the Hulluch road.

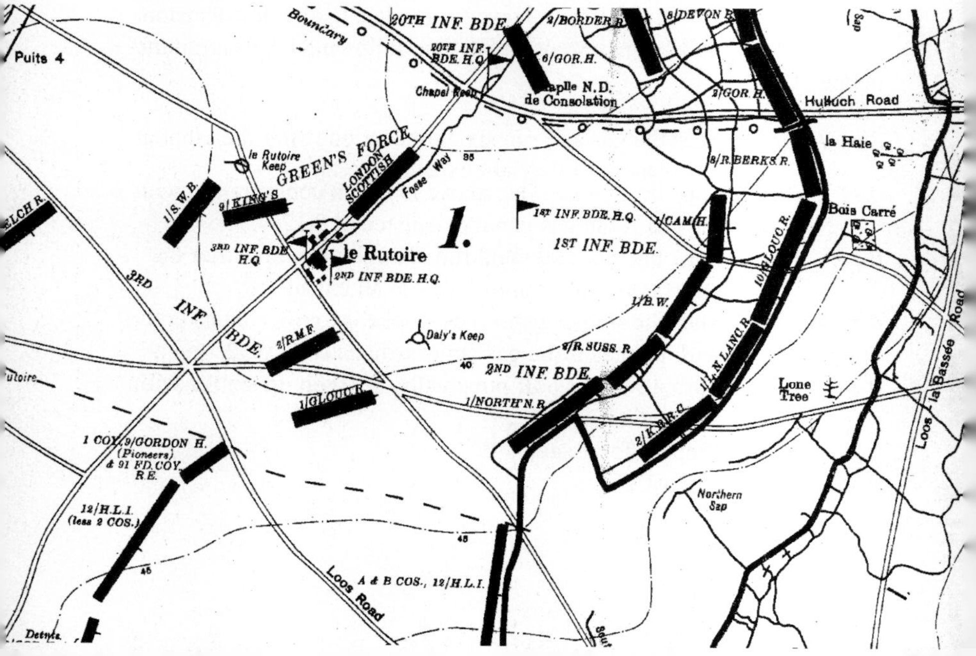

retaliated, firing blindly onto the Brigade's trenches. There were problems too in the gas trench, when leaky cylinders released concentrated clouds of gas, which drifted back over assembly trenches. Despite the setback, which caused a number of casualties amongst the Berkshires, the attack began as planned. Deep in the shattered Bois Carré, a machine-gun lay hidden, untouched by the artillery barrage. Unable to locate it for a time in the thick smoke, the Berkshires lost heavily crossing No Man's Land. Undeterred, they pressed on, eager to get to grips with their invisible assailant. The war diary describes the attack on Bois Carré:

> The fire of our artillery lifted and the Battalion advanced in quick time to assault the first line enemy trenches. The advance was opposed by heavy artillery and machine-gun fire, while the wire in front of the German trenches was found to be scarcely damaged, and it was in cutting a way through this obstacle that most of the regiment's heavy casualties occurred. Shrapnel and machine-gun combined to play havoc in our ranks, and an additional disaster was the blowing back of our gas, by the wind, into our own ranks.

> After a struggle the German first line was penetrated, and the trench found to be practically deserted, the enemy, apparently, having deserted it, merely leaving behind sufficient men to work the machine-guns. Mainly overland, but with some men working in the communication trench, our line advanced successively to the 2nd and 3rd German lines and met but slight opposition.

Artist's impression of a gas attack.

Although damaged by the bombardment, the wire caused considerable delays. IWM - Q28975

With the first line trench cleared the survivors were able to push on over the crest of the ridge, supported by the 1st Cameron Highlanders.

On the right of the brigade front, opposite La Haie copse, the 10th Gloucesters also experienced difficulties. As the gas officers began to open the stopcocks on the first batch of cylinders, it quickly became clear that the wind was not as strong as expected. Swirling clouds of choking gas and smoke engulfed the Gloucesters, incapacitating many. Even so, this setback failed to stall the men, as the war diary reports:

> The assault was carried out in 3 lines, frontage being BOIS CARREE inclusive to Point 39 in G.17.d. The attack was delivered at 06:30am with the accompaniment of gas and smoke. The wind was not quite favourable with the result that from the start several men were affected. Notwithstanding this drawback the three lines moved forward punctually to the moment, machine-guns accompanying.

A second machine-gun post, hidden in the tangled scrub that was once La Haie Copse, had escaped the artillery bombardment. It caused many casualties, firing blindly in great sweeps across the advancing lines before it was silenced. With grim determination the Gloucesters pushed on:

> The German's wire entanglement, which had been torn into gaps by bombardment, proved a considerable obstacle. The wind proving more favourable to the enemy than ourselves, in the smoke, direction was not properly maintained, but deflected to

the right. <u>Heavy resistance</u> encountered at the support and reserve German works, at the first, the enemy eventually evacuating these positions, and retreated towards HULLUCH. Our bombers suffered severely, their bombs in the main refusing to explode, the BROCK lighter having got wet with the rain, which fell in the early morning. Nevertheless the assault was pushed home with the utmost resolution over the 2nd German line into the third, and up the flanking communications trenches to eastwards.

The New Army men had proved that they could overcome the strongest of German positions in the most difficult of circumstances. However, at what cost? The Gloucesters war diary mourns the destruction of the Battalion, which had taken twelve months of training to prepare for its first battle:

1 Brigade's view of Hulluch as they crossed the summit of the Grenay Ridge. IWM - Q43119A

*The officers fell as the position of their bodies showed,
leading their men, and 16 out of 21 were lost. The bodies of our
dead indicated how they died, with faces to the enemy.*

The 1st Cameron Highlanders, following close in support, took over
the lead, capturing Gun Trench and three field guns. With the Germans
in full retreat, Lieutenant-Colonel Graeme's men pushed on over the
ridge, meeting little opposition. Ahead lay Hulluch, protected by an
undamaged belt of wire. It appeared that the village was deserted, but
Graeme was concerned that his men would be shot to pieces if he was
mistaken. Halting on the Lens Road to await the arrival of the 1st Black
Watch, the Camerons sent patrols forward to reconnoitre the ruins. At
09.10am Graeme sent a message to 1 Brigade headquarters;

*...mixed party of our brigade have captured a trench close to
Hulluch. Enemy reported to be retiring there.*

Unfortunately, the message gave an over-optimistic impression of the
situation. To the officers at brigade headquarters, it appeared as though
that the German Second Line had been breached and Hulluch taken. In
actual fact, as later research discovered, only thirty men entered the
village. Although they found the streets deserted, the small party of
men could do nothing but wait for reinforcements.

2 Brigade

2 Brigade, under Brigadier-General James Pollard, was on the right
of 1st Division's assault, with the 1st Loyal North Lancashires on the
left, the 2nd Kings Royal Rifle Corps on the right, the 2nd Royal
Sussex in support and the 1st Northamptonshires in reserve. The
Brigade's fifth battalion, the 1/9th King's (Liverpool) completed
Green's force behind the centre of Major-General Holland's front. Yet
again the brigade was at a disadvantage, holding the lower slopes of the
ridge. The only landmark was Lone Tree, which stood in No Man's
Land opposite the centre of the brigade. Two saps jutted out from the
German front line, one close to Lone Tree, and the second, Northern
Sap, faced the right flank of the brigade. The area immediately to the
right of the brigade was only lightly held. IV Corps plan had left an
intentional gap, about 500 metres wide, between the flanks of the 1st
and the 15th (Scottish) Division.

Even before zero hour 2 Brigade was in difficulties. During the
release of the gas, the wind changed direction, engulfing the assembly
trenches with a choking fog. On the left the assault companies of the
Loyal North Lancashires in the first line were decimated. As zero
approached most were laid in the bottom of the trenches, asphyxiated.

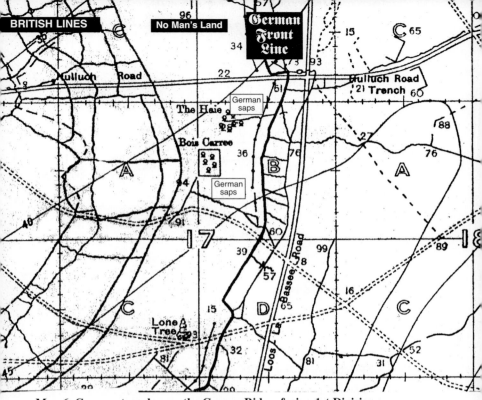

Map 6. German trenches on the Grenay Ridge, facing 1st Division.

Meanwhile, the Riflemen experienced similar difficulties. To make matters worse, the two 4" Stokes mortars employed to supplement the smoke screen were disabled at an early stage:

> *5.50am Gas turned on and began firing smoke shells from Stokes guns (These guns got done in. In one the copper collar burst and charge burst in the other, we got off about 30 rounds between the two). 6.00am The wind changed, all the gas blew back especially onto B coy. All ranks had smoke helmets on (old pattern ordered to be used). Consequently, most of B coy were gassed. Not all very bad but it had put them out of action. Reported to BDE. Ordered to attack.*

Both battalions ordered their support companies forward to replace the incapacitated men. With the front trench already congested with poisoned men, it was a difficult task. Many had clambered out of the trenches to escape the gas, taking cover behind the parados in the hope of finding clear air. With the minutes ticking by, it looked as though the assault would fail before it started. Realising that his assault battalions were in difficulty, Brigadier-General Pollard allowed a five minute delay to allow time to reorganise.

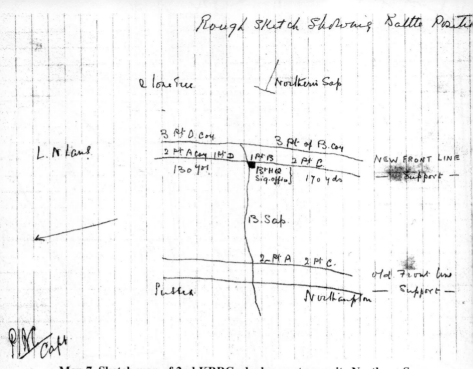

Map 7. Sketch map of 2nd KRRCs deployment opposite Northern Sap.

At 6.20am it appeared that the wind had changed again, and the gas officers considered it safe to release the last batch of cylinders. At 6.34am those still capable in the leading waves moved forward and they immediately came under fire. The Loyal North Lancashires were targeted by a machine-gun that had remained concealed near to Lone Tree. They also found it impossible to retain formation in the swirling clouds of smoke and gas;

> ...Owing to gas got mixed up and four lines advanced together, also we got mixed up with the KRRC on our right. We advanced up to the German wire but found it uncut and retired.

The 2nd King's Royal Rifle Corps were faced with the same difficulties. Another machine-gun hidden at the end of Northern Sap fired into the troops as they groped their way forward through the poisonous mist. Again they found that the artillery had failed to cut the wire entanglement:

> Could see nothing for smoke and gas between the lines - Very difficult to find direction. Most people choking. On reaching the wire it was discovered that it was not cut, being low and wide. On the left of the Battn troops started to go back. This left the right of the Battn in the air as there was a gap of 500 yards to our right unattacked. The Battn had to fall back.

50

Where possible the officers, in particular Colonel Sanderson of the Loyals, rallied their men for another attempt. By now the smoke was beginning to clear and as the men advanced for a second time they were hit by a heavy and accurate fire. As the Loyals diary reports, many officers were shot down as they urged their men forward:

> ...He (Colonel Sanderson) and the Adjutant, Captain Dever, were wounded, also 2/Lt P Goldie who was with them was killed. Officer casualties; 9 killed, 5 wounded, 2 missing. Captain Faulkner, Lts Levesey, Wharton and Healey all killed right on the German wire. Lt Warborough, MG officer, took his two guns practically up to German wire, he was killed. Lt Gardner, the other MG officer, went out on left flank with his two guns, nearly all his team was gassed and he carried a gun out himself with two men. He was gassed but came back to get ammunition and was told by Doctor to return to the rear, but he went and got more ammunition.

No Man's Land was strewn with over five hundred dead and wounded Loyals. Private Henry Kenny was one man who set about rescuing stricken men. Braving shrapnel and bullets he scoured the ground, eventually managing to carry six men back to the safety. As he handed the last man over the parapet Kenny was wounded in the neck, bringing his exploits to an end. Private Kenny returned to the front three months later and survived the war. In March 1916 his bravery was rewarded with the Victoria Cross. He went on to serve in the Local Defence Volunteers in World War Two and lived to the age of ninety.

Private Henry Kenny VC.

The situation was similar on the Rifle Corps front. The wire had remained intact and, with the smoke clearing, the survivors were pinned down in the open. Private George Peachment, aged only eighteen, was close to the German wire when he noticed that his company commander, Captain G R Dubs, was wounded. Rather than retiring with his comrades, Peachment crawled over to the stricken officer. Ignoring the bullets and refusing to take cover, Peachment tried to bandage Dubs' wounds. After being wounded himself in the chest by a bomb, Peachment began to drag the incapacitated officer to shelter. A rifle bullet ended the young man's life, his lifeless body was found slumped by his captain. As his citation for his Victoria Cross states,

Private George Peachment VC.

> He was one of the youngest men in his battalion, and

gave this splendid example of courage and sacrifice.
His grave was lost later in the war and Rifleman Peachment's name appears on the Dud Corner Memorial.

Having seen the Kings Royal Rifle Corps in difficulties, the company officers of the 2nd Royal Sussex decided to advance ahead of schedule. Ten minutes after the opening attack, three companies of the battalion went over the top. They too were met by a murderous fire and brought to a standstill in front of the wire. Sergeant Harry Wells took command of his platoon when his platoon officer fell. Leading the men forward to within fifteen metres of the wire, Wells seemed to live a charmed life. Major F W B Willett, one of the few surviving officers, described what happened in a letter written after the war:

> *Owing to the wire being entirely uncut, the assault failed, the battalion losing 19 officers and nearly 600 men in less than 15 minutes...Sergeant Wells three times rallied his men and led them against the wire under close and continuous machine-gun fire. During the third attempt Sergt. Wells and practically all the survivors of his platoon were killed.*

Sergeant Wells, a reservist and veteran of several battles, was posthumously awarded the Victoria Cross. His grave is situated in Dud Comer Cemetery, where many of his men are commemorated.

At first Brigadier-General Pollard was unable to see what was happening through the smoke clouds. However, as the minutes passed, by he learnt that three-quarters of his brigade had been broken. With scant reserves at hand, he frantically arranged for a renewed attack to take place in the hope of rallying the survivors in No Man's Land. It took nearly an hour to muster a meagre force who, with great difficulty, took up positions in the already crowded fire trench. Shortly before 8.00am, two companies of the 1st Northamptons and the last remaining company of the Sussex went over the top. The Northants war diary explains what happened:

> *A second attack was then ordered, the Sussex to advance on the left, centre on 'Lone Tree'. The Battalion, less 'A' Coy and parts of 'B', who were used for carrying ammunition, to attack on their right. This attack commenced about 9.00am. The men went forward well. 'D' Coy were able to get close to German wire entanglement which was found to be uncut. 'C' having a wide open piece of ground to traverse were unable to get so far forward and had heavy casualties, Lieut Jockey being mortally wounded. The line was unable to advance close enough to cut wire and remained lying out in open for two hours. Sussex on our*

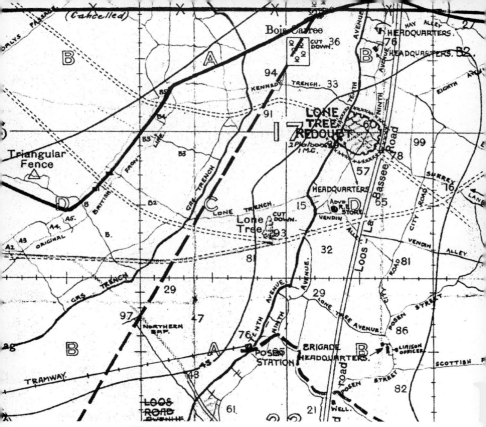

Map 8. Trench map of the Lone Tree area after the battle, note the Gas Trench and assembly trenches in front of the original front line.

> *left being in same predicament. This limited attack stood no chance of success, by now the smoke and gas had dispersed during the delay.*

Such a small force, advancing against an alert enemy, stood no chance. For a third time 2 Brigade was at standstill. Captain Anketell Read, one of the few surviving senior officers, realised that the only option left was to establish a firing line close to the German wire. Gathering together any able bodied men he could find, Read directed them forward. The 1st Northants war diary describes what happened:

> *Captain Read had very gallantly gone out to rally a party of about sixty men of different units who were retiring disorganised owing to the gas drifting back. The men were led forward again by him and took up a position south of Lone Tree, where they maintained themselves for some hours.*

Despite the fact that he was suffering for the effects of gas Captain Read tirelessly moved backwards and forwards along the line directing

53

Artist's impression of Captain Read leading stragglers back to the firing line.

fire and encouraging the men. As an obvious target, he eventually fell victim to sniper fire. Captain Anketell Read was posthumously awarded the Victoria Cross and his grave was eventually moved to Dud Corner Cemetery.

Captain Anketell Read VC.

By 8.30am Brigadier-General Pollard's Brigade was finished, having used all four of its battalions. No Man's Land was littered with dead and dying men, many others lay pinned down close to the German wire. If anyone moved they immediately drew the attention of every rifle in range, even so a few crawled or ran back to safety. Although reinforcements were on their way; it would, however, be some time before they were in a position to renew the attack.

Green's Force

Major-General Holland had six battalions waiting in reserve around Le Rutoire Farm. Two were grouped together under Lieutenant-Colonel Green, with orders to advance between the divergent attacks of 1 and 2 Brigades. 1st Division's Operational orders for Green's Force were brief:

> Its mission therefore is to watch for, and move forward to meet, any counter-attack which the enemy may attempt to push in between the 1st and 2nd Brigades. The CRA will assist in this mission by establishing a barrage 300 yards east of the road between Puits 14 bis and Hulluch, if and when the enemy launches a counter-attack.

54

Once Green's Force had taken the German Second Line between Hulluch and Bois Hugo, Brigadier-General H R Davies' 3 Brigade would take over the advance.

However, by 7.30am Major-General Holland's plan lay in tatters. Although 1 Brigade was closing on Hulluch, 2 Brigade was pinned down around Lone Tree. The first message from 2 Brigade arrived at divisional headquarters shortly after 8.00am;

2nd Brigade at first held up, but Sussex have now got through into German trenches

Based on this erroneous information, General Holland decided to alter his original plan in the hope of making up for lost time. If sufficient weight of numbers could be thrown behind 2 Brigade, the whole front could be cleared and he would be able to move forward 3 Brigade unobstructed. After instructing Brigadier-General Pollard to "push on with all speed" beyond Lone Tree, he ordered Colonel Green to:

Push forward your leading battalion as rapidly as possible in order to assist advance of 2nd Brigade

In fact both of Green's battalions, the 1/9th King's (Liverpool) and the 1/14th (London Scottish), left their assembly trenches. Almost at once they came under long-range fire from beyond Lone Tree. The London Scottish regimental history summarises the advance:

The London Scottish advanced in two lines of companies in two lines of platoons, A and D in the front line, B and C in the second. The attack of the 2nd Brigade having failed, and the smoke cleared away, the advance had to be made in full view of the enemy and under aimed fire. As soon as the companies began to move they came under shell and rifle fire and had to extend. Their casualties were heavy, but they advanced as if on parade, the Black Watch cheering as we passed.

At the head of the 1/9th Kings marched Lieutenant-Colonel Ramsey, carrying a wand, a device used to identify him as the commanding officer.

As Green's Force moved forward, Major-General Holland received a second message from the front, and for the first time 2 Brigade's plight came to light. He immediately sent an order to Colonel Green instructing his troops to attack at once, taking Brigadier-General Pollard's men forward. Meanwhile, Green's Force had reached the assembly trenches and they could see for themselves the situation around Lone Tree. The London Scottish war diary sums up the appalling circumstances:

Arrived at the front trenches, the force lay down behind the

Map 9. Summary of 1st Division's advance until 3.00pm. 1 Brigade is in front of Hulluch, while 2 Brigade remains pinned down at Lone Tree.

parados to await the capture of the German first line. Away to the left the 1st Brigade could be seen in the enemy's trenches but there was no sign of their bombing parties. Of the 2nd Brigade there was nothing to be seen but groups of dead and wounded out in front, and gassed and wounded men straggling. The shelling had now ceased, but the enemy kept up a brisk rifle fire, which rose like a tornado whenever a man moved. The London Scottish lost heavily during the advance, and they suffered still more losses during this time of waiting, for, on account of the gas, the troops could not enter the front trenches, and the low parapets behind which they lay afforded little cover. Several were hit beside the commanding officer, who lay, with Colonel Green, behind the front trench between the two battalions.

Here Green waited for further instructions, for it was obvious to him by now that his original orders were out-dated.

Chapter Five

15TH (SCOTTISH) DIVISION

46 Brigade's assault

46 Brigade, under the command of Brigadier-General Torquil Matheson, was on the left of 15th Division's assault. The brigade had two companies of the 12th Highland Light Infantry on the left, the 7th Kings Own Scottish Borderers in the centre and the 10th Scottish Rifles on the right. The remaining two companies of the 12th Highland Light Infantry and the 8th King's Own Scottish Borderers were in support.

Map 10. 15th (Scottish) Division's deployment north of the Lens road.

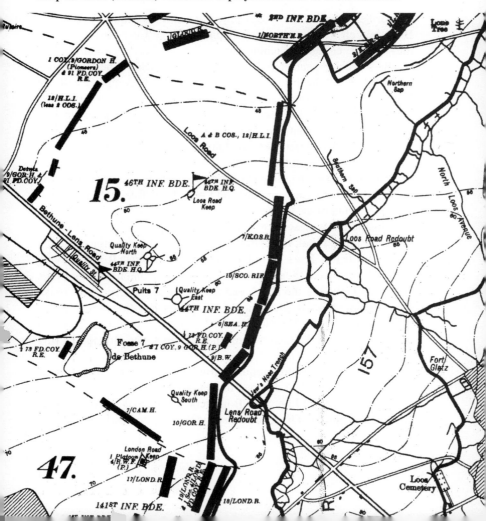

Artistic impression (minus the gas and smoke) of 46 Brigade's attack on Grenay Ridge.

Northern and Southern saps jutted out into No Man's Land on the Brigade's left flank. As previously discussed, IV Corps suspected that they might conceal machine-guns. Fearing heavy casualties, the planners decided against delivering a frontal attack on the 500 metres sector north of the brigade. Instead 'A' and 'B' companies of the Highland Light Infantry under Captain P W Torrance would attack the sector by bombing. Torrance's men would accompany the advance as far as the German front line, they would then turn north, bombing their way up the German trenches. By doing so the HLI could outflank the two saps and link with the right flank of 1st Division.

The 7th King's Own Scottish Borderers were positioned astride the track that ran between Vermelles and Loos. Loos Road Redoubt stood directly in front of the Borderers, near the summit of the Grenay Ridge. The position was heavily wired and consisted of interlinked strong points designed for all round defence in case the line on either side fell into enemy hands. Jew's Nose Trench faced the Scottish Rifles, curving in an arc away from their line as it followed the contours of the ridge. In the weeks before the attack engineers had dug a series of Russian saps (shallow tunnels which could be opened into trenches in a few hours) up the slope. They were turned into a new front line, only 200 metres away from the German trenches. Even so, 46 Brigade faced a stiff task.

At 5.50am the gas programme started and it soon became obvious that either the wind had dropped or changed, causing the gas to settle on the Scottish front line. The Borderers Regimental History gives a graphic description of the conditions endured by the Lowland Brigade:

HEAD OF
SOUTHERN SAP

The 7th went over the top. In itself it meant a physical as well as moral effort. Half smothered in their smoke helmets they had to scramble out of the 250 yards of fire trench in which they crowded, get through the gaps cut in the wire, and spread out to something over 400 yards of frontage - and this, heavily laden and with rifles with fixed bayonets...As can be imagined, things did not go to clockwork. Men were affected by gas. It was Hobson's choice - To be half choked for want of air, or wholly choked in the attempt to get it.

On the left of the brigade the gas settled in the HLI's trenches, by the time zero hour arrived many of Captain Torrance's men were asphyxiated. With the battalion machine-guns covering their exposed left flank, the depleted rifle sections led the bombers across No Man's Land. 'B' company, on the left, made for Southern Sap in the hope of using it as cover. However, it was only a mere scrape in the ground and German machine-guns extracted their retribution. Every officer and sergeant was hit as they led their men forward across the exposed ground. The survivors broke into the German trenches, but were too few to bomb northwards. At 7.15am the machine-gun officer led his four gun teams across the bullet swept ground to reinforce the beleaguered force. One in three became casualties, but the survivors managed to drag three guns into position. Private Ramage was conspicuous in the cool and able manner in which he handled his gun, driving off several counter-attacks.

At noon Second Lieutenant Watson brought the 6th Cameron Highlanders bombers across, with a fresh supply of bombs. His men had limited success in bombing northwards, but were unable to reach

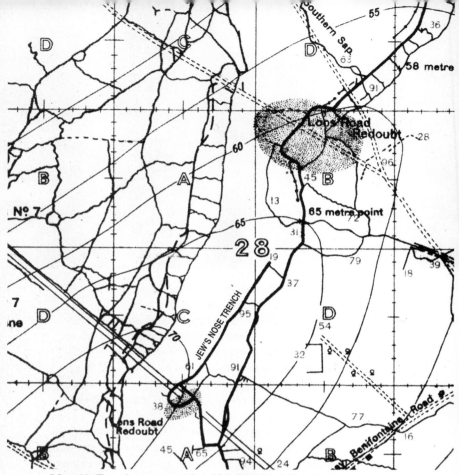

Map 11. Trench map covering 15th Division's front, the shading around the two redoubts denotes broken ground cut up by artillery fire.

1st Division. Only when Ritter's men in front of 2 Brigade surrendered was contact made, over eight hours after zero.

In the 7th KOSB sector the gas clouds engulfed the assault troops and for a few minutes it seemed as though the advance would falter. Second Lieutenant Martin Young called to his piper, Daniel Laidlaw:

'for God's sake, Laidlaw, pipe 'em together'. Laidlaw climbed onto the parapet, pulled back his smoke helmet and struck up the 'Blue Bonnets'. The sound of the pipes rallied the Borderers and those still able to move mounted the parapet. Marching forward, they were met by the deadly chatter of machine-gun fire. Two guns in the redoubt conducted two sweeps along the ranks of Borderers, killing and wounding many. Piper Laidlaw was hit by shrapnel but continued to limp forward, changing the tune to 'The Standard on the Braes o' Mar'. A second shell brought the piper down, and mortally wounded Lieutenant Young. Undeterred the Scots pushed on, clambering over the broken wire and onto the redoubt. The battalion bombers rushed forward taking care of the machine-guns, and many Germans were captured in their dugouts.

Piper Daniel Laidlaw was awarded the Victoria Cross for his bravery, the first awarded to a New Army soldier. He survived the war, re-enacting his deeds in two films. He died in 1950. Lieutenant Young was buried in Noeux-les-Mines Cemetery.

The 10th Scottish Rifles, on the right of the Brigade, came under heavy machine-gun fire from Jew's Nose Trench as they advanced across No Man's Land. Three company officers and six subalterns were

Piper Daniel Laidlaw VC.

Loos Road Redoubt, a maze of battered trenches and broken wire.
IWM - Q28985

killed before the wire. Fortunately the artillery had managed to cut the German wire, and without delay the Rifles stormed the trench with bayonet and bomb. In spite of gas and heavy casualties, the Lowland Brigade had proved themselves.

Unabated, the KOSB's and the Scottish Rifles pushed forward over the crest as fast as the wet clay would allow them. Ahead lay the Loos valley, enshrouded in smoke and mist. The only consolation was that the air was now clear enough to breathe and many rolled up or discarded their smoke helmets. Moving steadily forward across the valley, 46 Brigade's advance was relatively uneventful, although the discovery of an abandoned six-gun battery north of the village raised the men's morale. The men found it eerie as they advanced across the sodden fields unopposed, the sounds of battle raging to the south. As the Scottish Rifles approached the north-eastern outskirts of Loos, machine-gun fire struck the battalion in the flank. Many Cameronians turned to face the threat and were drawn into the village via the Loos-Hulluch Road. As they worked their way south they became embroiled in 44 Brigade's battle for the ruins.

Meanwhile, it appeared as though the battlefield was deserted to the left of the brigade. The 7th KOSB sent patrols north through the mist in the search of the 1st Division, but they returned having found no one. As the men started to climb the far slope of the valley, the mist cleared and for the first time it was possible to see a recognisable landmark, Puits 14 Bis and its unmistakable chimney. At 9.15am the Borderers lined the Lens highway, as a message from Major T Glenny confirms;

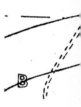

> Have reached 300 yards South of Puits 14 Bis. Going strong. Have halted for another blow as our artillery are firing a bit short. Shall push on again immediately.

The remainder of 10th Scottish Rifles waited alongside the Borderers while events developed on Hill 70 to the south. A little later the remnants of the 12th HLI and three companies of the 8th KOSB reinforced the position.

44 Brigade's attack

44 Brigade, under the command of Brigadier-General Montagu Wilkinson, was on the right of 15th Division's attack, with the 8th Seaforth Highlanders on the left and the 9th Black Watch on the right.

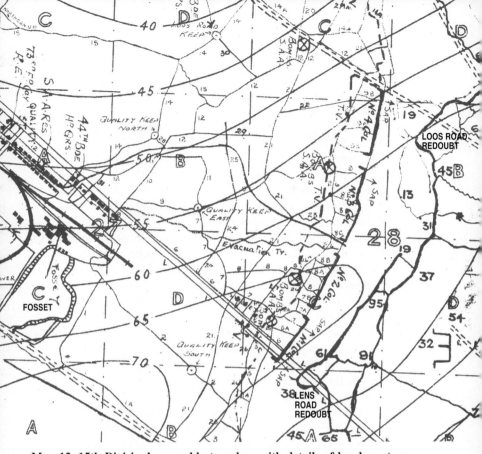

Map 12. 15th Division's assembly trenches, with details of headquarters and ammunition stores.

The 7th Cameron Highlanders were positioned in support, with the 10th Gordon Highlanders in reserve. The Seaforths faced the southern section of Jew's Nose trench, which followed the contour of the ground south until it met Lens Road Redoubt (or Jew's Nose Redoubt). The redoubt was built on the summit of the ridge, blocking the Lens Road. Directly opposite, the 9th Black Watch huddled in their assembly trenches only 200 metres away.

On the Seaforths front the gas cloud caused consternation in the assembly trenches. Minutes ticked by before order was restored and 'A' and 'C' companies began clambering into the open. One of the first casualties was 'A' company's CO, Captain Alec Ravenhill, shot dead as he knelt on the parapet helping his men to climb out:

> *The men passed through gaps in our own wire, and formed up beyond in good order then bore down steadily on the German*

63

wire. The German resistance broke before the shock of the assault; and with great rapidity progress was continued to the second German line....The speed made by the attack had been phenomenal, indeed; and the success attained promised to exceed the most sanguine expectations. The first line trenches had been taken in some ten to fifteen minutes. These had not been strongly held, and the garrison, which had met our men with machine-gun fire, did not await the assault.

Despite having suffered over one hundred casualties, including Lieutenant-Colonel Thomson, the adjutant and all four company commanders, the Seaforths overran Jew's Nose Trench.

On the 9th Black Watch front the gas failed to assist the advance and the battalion suffered a number of casualties before zero:

...At the hour received the enemy commenced a very heavy bombardment of our trenches. The wind not being of sufficient strength a portion of the gas came back into our trenches at the hour called for assaulting.

At zero hour the men climbed out of the trenches and formed up ready to advance. Almost at once the two machine-guns in Lens Road Redoubt began traversing the lines of Highlanders. One observer recalls how the Black Watch were unstoppable:

No one present will ever forget that attack. As one the leading two platoons of 'A' Company leapt on the parapet and, making their way through the British wire, steadily advanced toward the German front line, followed by the remainder of the Battalion at regular intervals. It seemed impossible to realise that these lines of disciplined soldiers had been, twelve short months before, almost all civilians. Perfect steadiness prevailed, regardless of the heavy fire which, coming more especially from the Lens Road Redoubt, swept the ground over which they had to cross. There was no shouting or hurry; the men moved in quick time, picking up their dressing as if on ceremonial parade. The distance to be crossed varied from 80 to 200 yards and, despite the fierce fire, not a line wavered or stopped.

The 9th Black Watch stormed onto the redoubt, the battalion bombers leading the way. Yet again it was found that many of the Germans had fled at the first sign of gas. With the troublesome machine-guns silenced the advance could continue. As the regimental history reports, the battalion had suffered grievous losses, in particular amongst officers:

Within five minutes both the German front and support lines

Tower Bridge overlooks the centre of Loos. IWM - Q43113

had been taken, but at what a cost. Three of the company commanders, Major Henderson and Captains Graham and Bell, together with Lieutenants Henderson-Hamilton, Creighton, Cameron and Millar had been killed, together with all four company sergeant-majors and over 200 other ranks; while Captain McLeod, nearly all the remaining officers and a large number of other ranks had been wounded. As he lay on the ground, Major Henderson's last words to his company were, "keep going".

Moving swiftly forward over the brow of the ridge the men of the two Highland battalions ran down the steep slope towards Loos, close on the heels of the retreating Germans. Time was of the essence; a delay would allow the garrison stationed in Loos to man the Loos defence line on the outskirts. Again the Seaforths lost a considerable number of men cutting a way through the wire covering the Loos Defence Line. A single machine-gun in Fort Glatz caused many casualties before it was silenced by the battalion bombers. Fortunately, the rest of the garrison had been taken completely by surprise, many of them struggling to get ready for action. Only a handful of wild shots were fired from the men billeted in the houses. As the Seaforths war diary explains, the battalion split into two before it entered the village:

> *Machine-guns in front of the village were put out of action and then automatically all bombers were withdrawn from the left and put on the right flank for bomb fighting in the streets...The second line which was close into and covered Loos itself was taken with almost equal rapidity and the garrison withdrew into the town, or fled back to lines of defence further in rear.*

Meanwhile a single machine-gun post carefully concealed in the village cemetery managed to traverse the Black Watch before the London Irish, advancing to the right of the Black Watch, silenced it. Close to the wire a brutal incident incensed the Highlanders:

> *Second Lieutenant A Sharp was killed at the second German line. A German Officer had come up and surrendered to him at which 2nd Lt Sharp ordered his men not to fire at him - when a German soldier standing behind his officer treacherously killed him.*

By 7.00am, 44 Brigade was beginning to enter the maze of streets, becoming engaged in a fierce struggle. The Scots charged into the ruins, throwing aside barricades the defenders had hastily built across the streets. Finding themselves trapped, the Germans barricaded

The route taken by the 9th Black Watch and the London Irish as they entered Loos. IWM - Q28987

Emotive drawing depicting Scottish troops saving women and children.

themselves in their billets and began firing at the passing Scots. The enraged men spilt into groups, smashing their way through doors and throwing bombs through windows. They were unstoppable, and in many cases the Germans surrendered without a fight. Dozens of prisoners were hauled from the houses and ferried to the rear. Occasionally terrified civilians were brought out of the ruins, and quickly shepherded to safety. What is remarkable is that the Scots never had training for this type of warfare. Nevertheless, in record time the northern part of the village was cleared by the 8th Seaforths:

> *Many Germans were accounted for and many were taken prisoners from the rooms and cellars of the houses. A German battery of field guns was taken in the course of the advance, the Commander of the Battery being shot by Sgt R MacPhail of 'D' Coy.*

While the street fighting raged on, the left of the battalion followed an easier route:

> *The remainder of the Bn moved with its lines extending to the North of the town and kept pushing forwards. At places losses were severe until the bombers had cleared houses from which*

machine-guns were firing, and stopped the enemy's firing from the flank. The work done by the bombers in facilitating the advance was, indeed, invaluable.

Many of the Black Watch were funnelled into the village along the Grenay Road, entering the square by the church (after the war Loos Church was rebuilt in a different location, the original, smaller, structure stood on the edge of the square, where the war memorial is now). Again the assaulting troops broke up into small groups, bursting into houses, taking prisoners and rescuing civilians, the majority of whom were women and children. By 8.30am advanced parties of the Seaforths and the Black Watch, now intermingled with the support battalion, the 10th Gordon Highlanders, began to make their way out of the ruins. Many however, continued to fight on in the ruins.

Lieutenant-Colonel Sandilands, CO of the support battalion, the 7th Camerons, was taken by surprise by the speed of the advance. By the time he reached the crest of the ridge his men had moved off ahead of schedule;

I went straight to our original front trench but, however, I could not make out very clearly what was the situation so I proceeded to G,28, c.9.1. of the German second line. On arrival

Map 13. Trench map covering 15th Division's advance through Loos and onto Hill 70.

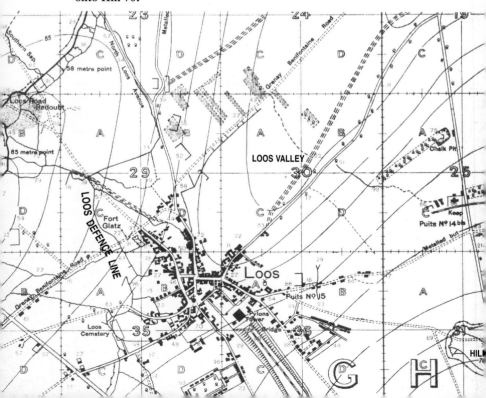

there halted to make a detailed reconnaissance. It could not then have been much more than 8 a.m. To my astonishment there were scarcely any signs of my own regiment in the immediate vicinity; they were all streaming through the German lines, into the houses of Loos. On my left I very soon distinguished the lines of 15th Division troops ascending the slope towards Puits No. 14 bis.

Moving quickly into the village, Sandilands was met with a scene of destruction. He set up his headquarters near the church and set about trying to establish contact with his men. The report given in the Camerons war diary paints a vivid picture of the vicious nature of street fighting:

In LOOS itself there were still parties going about bombing and bayoneting Germans running out of houses, and also taking prisoners. I sheltered behind a strongly built house close to LOOS church, but was heavily shelled and went in search of cellars. I found one which was occupied by Germans, who were killed, and this was used as my headquarters for a quarter of an hour. When one of my men with a Vermoral sprayer (used to combat gas) came along I sent him to the lower cellar of the house, where a German officer was found still telephoning to the enemy. He was killed.

Meanwhile the mopping up operation continued all around. All over the village groups of men worked their way through the ruins searching for Germans. Sergeant Findlay, leading No. 11 Platoon of the Pioneer Battalion the 10th Gordon Highlanders, came under machine-gun fire

Ruins and wreckage in the village.

2/Lt J Bruce-Wood.

from one strongly held house. With the help of an unknown Cameron his small party bombed their way forward capturing fifty prisoners. Second Lieutenant J Bruce-Wood, 10th Gordons, and his men eventually escorted 275 Germans into captivity. They then returned with desperately needed ammunition. In some cases the Germans had booby-trapped strategic buildings, but in the chaos and confusion they had failed to detonate the charges. Major E B Blogg, 4th London Field Company RE, was awarded the DSO for defusing a mine designed to demolish the church.

In the rush to advance many Germans were overlooked and throughout the day snipers shot at the unwary Scots as they carried out their duties. One particular incident invited admiration from all quarters. Captain F A Bearn, the Black Watch's medical officer, had set up his aid post in a shop owned by Emilienne Moreau's mother. Bearn later described to his superior officer how young Emilienne came to the soldiers' assistance:

This girl, who is only 17 years old, was living with another woman in a shop at Loos in the Church Square. These premises were taken as a regimental aid post by Captain Bearn and these two women spent the whole day and night in helping to carry in the wounded and carry out the dead, also preparing food and coffee for all, refusing payment. This work was done continuously for twenty-four hours. When the British troops were making effective efforts to dislodge two German snipers from the next house, who were firing on the stretcher bearers, this young girl seized a revolver from an officer and went into the back of a house and fired two shots at the snipers. She came back saying, "C'est fini", and handed the revolver back to the officer. It is uncertain if the two shots actually killed the men but the diversion in the rear enabled our men to make an entrance in front. Captain Bearn states: "I saw many examples of cool courage that day but none that excelled hers".

Emiliene Moreau.

Two months later Mademoiselle Moreau was awarded the Croix de Guerre and the Military Cross by General de Sailly at Versailles. The village school is named in memory of the brave young lady who once taught the children of Loos.

Small parties and isolated snipers continued to hide out in the ruins,

The inhabitants of Bethune turn out to view captured guns. IWM - Q28963

harassing the Scots as they moved about the village. Eventually on 28th September a systematic search was organised, finally clearing the ruins of Germans. The searchers were also surprised to discover a number of field guns buried under the rubble.

Advance onto Hill 70

By 9.00am, 44 Brigade, or rather a mixed body of men, began to collect on the east side of the village. Even though morale was high, the brigade was suffering in two respects. The confused fighting amongst the ruins had caused the various battalions to become very intermingled and there was no time to stop and reorganise. The second problem was officer casualties; very few senior officers were still standing. Many of those who had survived had lost contact with their subordinates in the village. Despite the fact that General Wilkinson's brigade had ceased to be a coherent formation, his men kept going, mindful of their orders to 'push on'. Observers on the Grenay ridge watched eagerly as a large crowd of men, about 1,500 strong, made their way to the summit of Hill 70.

The garrison of Hill 70 redoubt, seeing that they were outnumbered, ran south towards Cité St Laurent. With a rousing cheer the Scots followed in hot pursuit. Unfortunately, this pulled the direction of the advance to the south, rather than east as ordered. The diary of the 8th Seaforth Highlanders describes the advance over the crest:

> In advancing the village of LOOS and Crassier behind the pylons seemed to exercise a bad fascination on the firing line. The line also was inclined to the right by the desire to get in touch with the London Division. The result was that the Seaforth Highlanders and Black Watch mixed up with the Gordons and Camerons left the German work at H31 Central on their left and advanced on the CITE St LAURENT rather than the CITE St AUGUSTE. The right of the line emerged directly on Puits 12, where its further advance was impossible owing to the fact that our heavy artillery was shelling the mine and apparently searching for a battery right up against which we had arrived and which continued to fire in our immediate neighbourhood until one gun was knocked out by one of our shells. As advance was obviously impossible here the line then inclined to the left and directed its attack against a position extending from PUITS 12 to the DYNAMITIERE at N.1.B.1.2. The Dynamitiere was strongly held by Machine-Guns and our guns began wasting their ammunition at this point. This seemed to strike the line, for after a bit it apparently wavered.

Men from the Loos garrison, reinforced by a detachment from the 22nd Reserve Regiment, barred the way forward. From behind the uncut belt of wire they returned fire, bringing the Scots advance to an abrupt halt. A second wave composed of the 7th Camerons and 10th Gordons was caught unawares as it approached Cité St Laurent:

> We advanced right over the moor on to Hill 70 and some officer told us that the Camerons and Black Watch were occupying the village in front and we pushed over to support them.
>
> When we got over the crest we found a number of machine guns firing on men in front. Lieut. Christison joined our line and instructed the machine gunners to stop firing, as they were firing on the Black Watch and Camerons. We then proceeded down the hill towards the village in front when a murderous machine gun and rifle fire opened on us. Instead of it being the Black Watch and Camerons as we thought, we found it to be the retreating enemy who ran down a road through houses and manned a

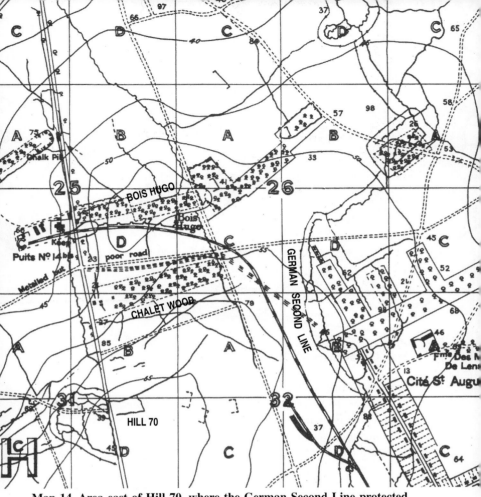

Map 14. Area east of Hill 70, where the German Second Line protected Cité St Auguste.

trench, which was heavily barbed wired.

We advanced until we were about 150 yards from this trench and Lieut. Robertson, who was in command of the line, gave us orders for the men to make head cover. The enemy's fire was causing a great deal of casualties on the line.

Meanwhile, on the left, 46 Brigade met a similar fate. Seeing a number of men disappearing into Cité St Auguste, the leading wave mistook them for Scots. They were in fact German artillerymen manhandling their guns back from the exposed slope. With a cheer, Brigadier-General Matheson's men ran forward to catch up. Waiting behind an uncut wire entanglement were a company of 22nd Reserve Regiment who had been roused from their billets by the noise of battle. Their fire

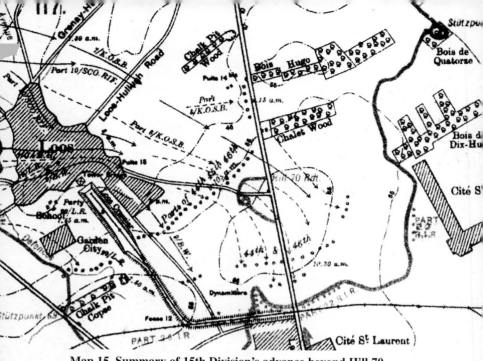

Map 15. Summary of 15th Division's advance beyond Hill 70.

brought 46 Brigade's charge to an abrupt halt.

> *When they crossed the crest of Hill 70, they found several machine guns in action and a line of KOSB on their left. They joined up and advanced down the hill. There seemed to be some doubt as to whether there was any of our troops in front. Suddenly they found a strong line of barbed wire concealed in the grass and at the same time a heavy machine gun and rifle fire was opened on them. They lay down and tried to make some cover.*

15th Division's advance was finished, its force spent. Around eight or nine hundred men lay pinned down in an arc, facing east towards Cite St Auguste and south towards Cite St Laurent. Attempts were made to get to grips with the Germans and many tried to push forward by short rushes. There was little hope, for each time they moved the Germans opened a heavy crossfire. There was no other option but to dig in and wait for reinforcements. All across the bare slope men desperately tried to scratch hollows in the ground.

74

Chapter Six

47th (LONDON) DIVISION

141 Brigade

141 Brigade, commanded by Brigadier-General William Thwaites, held the left-hand sector of the 47th Division. The brigade faced a difficult task, for having cleared the front trench the men would have to advance over half a mile down the gentle slope towards the southern outskirts of Loos. At the bottom of the slope was the Loos Defences, which ran through the village cemetery. Thwaites chose to attack with only one battalion, the 1/18th London (London Irish), which would halt on the defence line. The two support battalions, the 1/19th London (St Pancras) and the 1/20th London (Blackheath and Woolwich) would then advance through the southern outskirts of Loos. The 1/19th London's objective were the 'Mine Buildings and Crassier-Puits 15',

Map 16. 47th (London) Division's dispositions at zero hour.

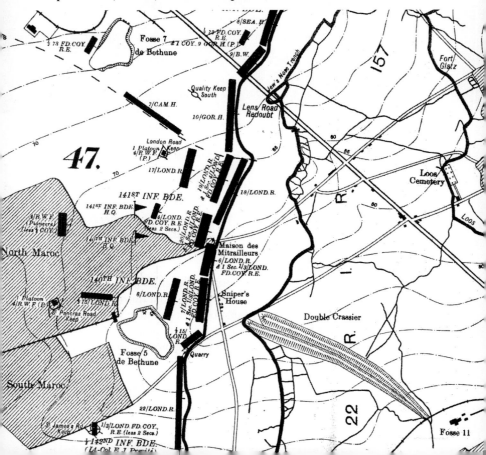

In places the British artillery completely destroyed the German wire.

the pit where most of the men in the village had worked prior to the war. The pithead tower was affectionately called the 'Tower Bridge' and the adjacent slagheap, a huge wall of ash, was known as the 'Grandstand'. Meanwhile, the 1/20th London would skirt past the south of the village, clearing an isolated estate of miners' cottages known as 'Welwyn Garden City'. After clearing the houses they would head up the slopes to Chalk Pit Copse and the strongpoint known to the Germans as Stutzpunkt 69.

As soon as the gas started the Germans began shelling the brigade's trenches, supplemented by rifle fire from the front line trench. Despite this attention, the shrapnel only burst one gas cylinder; it did, however, mean that the men had to put their gas helmets on early. For once the gas moved in the direction it was supposed to, moving slowly down the

slopes engulfing the German trenches. At zero hour the advance started without delay and platoon after platoon moved forward quickly to climb the ladders. Men of the leading platoon on the right dribbled a football between them, aiming to score a 'goal' in the German trench. Patrick Macgill, a well-known author, was a stretcher-bearer with the London Irish. His record of the attack portrays the thoughts of a soldier going over top:

It was now a grey day, hazy and moist, and the thick clouds of pale yellow smoke curled high in space

Chlorine gas brought new horrors to the Western Front.

Patrick Macgill.

and curtained the dawn off from the scene of war. The word was passed along "London Irish lead on to assembly trench". The assembly trench was in front, and the scaling ladders were placed against the parapet, ready steps to death, as someone remarked. I had a view of the men swarming up the ladders when I got there, their bayonets held in steady hands, and at a little distance off a football swinging by its whang from a bayonet standard.

The company were soon out in the open marching forward. The enemy's guns were busy, and the rifle and Maxim bullets ripped the sandbags. The infantry fire was wild but of slight intensity. The enemy could not see the attacking party. But, judging by the row, it was hard to think that men could weather the leaden storm in the open.

I went to the foot of the ladder and got hold of a rung. A soldier in front was clambering across. Suddenly he dropped backwards and bore me to the ground; the bullet had caught him in the forehead. I got to my feet to find a stranger in grey uniform coming down the ladder. He reached the floor of the trench and put up his hands when I looked at him.

Rifle and machine-gun fire met the London Irish as they advanced, but due to the effective smoke screen, much of it was wild or high. Within minutes the German trench was entered and a fierce hand-to-hand struggle ensued. Many Germans were in the process of manning the

141 Brigade's view of the village, Loos cemetery is to the left. IWM - Q37564

front trench when the Irish reached them; the slower ones were caught in their dugouts. Taken by surprise and outnumbered, the surviving Germans soon turned and ran only to fall victim to overhead machine-gun fire. Brigadier Thwaites had placed six Maxims in reserve to fire indirectly over the attacking waves in one of the earliest attempts at this type of supporting barrage. At 7.00am Major W H Matthews reported that the London Irish had crossed the Bethune - Lens highway near Valley Crossroads and was moving towards Loos Cemetery.

By now the smoke screen was dispersing fast, exposing the advancing London Irish to the few Germans holding the cemetery. A single machine-gun, concealed in a crypt, fired until the last moment, causing fearful casualties. Many were struck down as the men equipped with wire-cutters forced a way through the uncut wire. Their task complete, the Irish halted, allowing the support battalions to push on to the final objective.

The 1/19th (St Pancras) London, following close behind the left of the London Irish, were caught by heavy enfilading fire from their left while crossing No Man's Land. Here, the section of line immediately south of Lens Road Redoubt bent back, taking advantage of the flat crest. It was deemed unwise to cross the wide stretch of No Man's Land in case the redoubt held out for some time before it was captured. The London Irish had entered the German trench before the unmolested section was manned. Unfortunately, by the time the St Pancras men started to cross No Man's Land, two machine-gun crews had manned their guns. They quickly realised that there were no men to their front and they were free to engage the inviting target crossing to their left. Casualties were heavy, Lieutenant-Colonel Harold Collinson-Morley was mortally wounded, the adjutant and many other officers were hit, a loss that would hamper the battalion severely. Captain A P Hamilton was seriously wounded but refused to be taken to safety. Instead he remained in the German second line organising the consolidation of the trench. He eventually had to be ordered back to receive medical attention, and was awarded the Military Cross for his devotion to duty.

The battalion headed for Valley Crossroads, reaching the cemetery just as the German batteries in Cité St Laurent found their range. From here on they took the lead, moving into the southern outskirts of Loos Crassier. After ripping down the protective wire netting fence, the St Pancras men were able to secure the area around Tower Bridge. They then skirted the northern end of the Grandstand, advancing up the slope behind the Scots. At its eastern end 'C' Company halted, having

The Grandstand looms over the southern outskirts of Loos. IWM - Q43114

reached its objective. They were able to make contact with a platoon of the 1/20th London that had established itself across the end of the Crassier. Here they waited for the rest of the battalion to join them. They were to be disappointed.

The remaining companies, by now virtually leaderless, had become intermingled with the 9th Black Watch. Some were swept along with the Scots and did not manage to rejoin the battalion until after the battle. The majority stayed in the village, becoming embroiled in the house clearing operation. Without their officers to order them forwards, the men naturally dealt with any German that fired on them. Lieutenant F L Pusch, the bombing officer, received a serious facial wound early on. Despite the pain, he went alone into an occupied house taking seven prisoners. Amongst the ruins the St Pancras men recovered a 77mm field gun and large quantities of ammunition. The battalion's losses had been grievous: 14 officers and nearly 350 other ranks.

Meanwhile, the 1/20th London, under Lieutenant-Colonel A B Hubback, had managed to reach the Loos defence line without serious loss. Advancing on the right of the 1/19th London, the battalion passed to the south of the cemetery and swung southeast towards Welwyn Garden City. From their positions in the Chalk Pit the men of the 26th Regiment watched and waited:

The lines came past the cemetery and then turned towards us.
During the moments when the cloud and mist lifted, great masses

of troops were now visible all along the front, the leading lines running, and those behind following at a walk; so many were there that it looked like a great trek. Those immediately in front of our position were not, however, clearly seen till within a hundred yards of our entanglement, and from their headdress we realised that the British were upon us. Line after line now rapidly approached in short rushes, whilst to our right we could see more masses pouring into Loos village.

Map 17. Street plan of Loos, the village defence line runs between Fort Glatz and the cemetery.

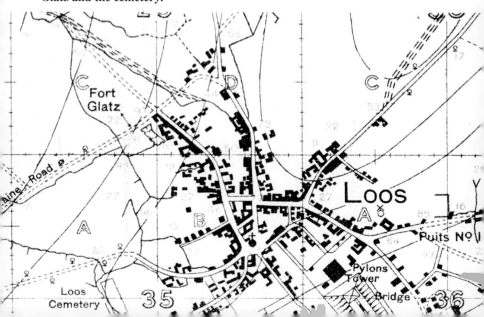

Welwyn Garden City was taken without a fight. As Lieutenant-Colonel Hubback set up his headquarters in one of the houses, he proudly watched as his men set to work:

> *The work of consolidation was proceeded with and the houses in the GARDEN CITY were put in a state of defence. The captured positions were maintained throughout the day. The attack was carried out with the greatest possible coolness and steadiness of all ranks could not have been surpassed. The result of the preparation was most apparent as on arrival at the GARDEN CITY each man knew exactly where to go.*

Meanwhile, Captain G Williams led 'A' company up the bare slope towards the final objective, Chalk Pit and the adjacent copse. Again resistance was light and before long the small quarry was taken along with two 85mm field guns. Attempts to take the copse failed. Most of the battalion grenadiers were by now dead or injured, and without trained bombers it was impossible to secure the copse. Throughout the morning Williams persisted, but each time his men were driven back by two machine-guns. The Germans also had a concealed Belgian field gun, which was able to fire over open sights every time the St Pancras men charged forwards. Around midday a detachment of Germans from the 27th Regiment reinforced the copse, and throughout the afternoon

The Chalk Pit can be seen on the slopes below Puits 12, Welwyn Garden City is in the foreground. IWM - Q43115

'A' Company grimly held onto the Chalk Pit.

By 9.00am 141 Brigade had secured the majority of its objectives, (all except Chalk Pit Copse), and was in the process of consolidating its position in case of counter-attack. Owing to the high number of officer casualties, Lieutenant-Colonel Hubback was instructed to take command of the 1/19th London as well as his own battalion. The reserve battalion, the 1/17th (Poplar and Stepney Rifles) London, sent one company under Major F E Evans to support Hubback's position in Chalk Pit Copse. The men dug in and strengthened their positions, and throughout the afternoon efforts were made to organise a defensive line. Brigadier-General Thwaite's men had achieved a tremendous success, clearing a difficult position in spite of heavy losses. All they had to do now was wait for reinforcements to arrive.

140 Brigade

140 Brigade, under the command of Brigadier-General Gerald Cuthbert, held the centre sector of the 47th Division. It would, however, form the right sector of the Division's assault on the extreme right of IV Corps' breakthrough. Its plan placed 1/6th (Rifles) London on the left, the 1/7th (City) London on the right with the 1/8th (Post Office Rifles) London in support and the 1/15th (Prince of Wales' Own Civil Service Rifles) London in reserve.

The 1/6th London had to advance down the bare slope 400 metres

before they reached the German trenches. They would then press on across the valley south of Loos village, eventually consolidating the German support line astride the main Lens highway. From this commanding position Lieutenant-Colonel Faux's men could prevent any counter-attacks from the direction of Cité St Pierre. Meanwhile, Lieutenant Colonel Mildren's 1/7th London faced an arduous task. Although No Man's Land was narrow on their front, the advance would be overlooked by the Double-Crassier. The German front line ran north from the slagheap at the foot of a long slope. Having taken the front trench, the left of the battalion would press on to the support line alongside the City Battalion. The right company had to scale the steep slopes of Double Crassier, capturing the trench that ran along its crest. The capture of the slagheap fell to Major Bill Casson's 'A' Company; without it 47th Division's position, and ultimately IV Corps' flank, would be exposed.

On the night before the attack the heavily laden assault troops filed into the trenches in complete darkness, while artillery shells screamed overhead. The two leading companies were packed tightly into the

Map 18. 47th Division's assembly trenches; note Fosse 5 behind the British lines, the slagheap used by artillery observers.

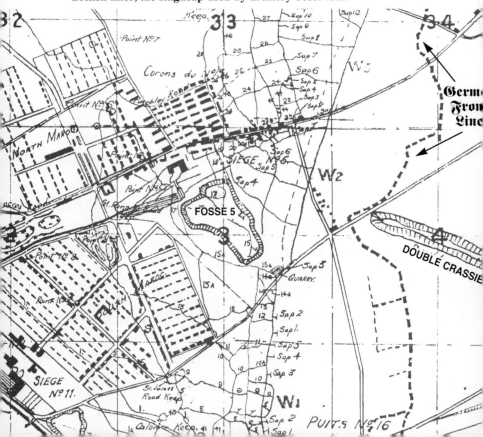

front trench, leading men to the left of the ladders, second company to the right. As dawn approached the men of the Special Brigade went to work releasing the gas. Wind direction and speed turned out to be favourable on the brigade front and the thick clouds rolled slowly into the valley below. The war diary of the 1/6th London vividly describes how the 'Cast Iron Sixth' advanced:

> At 6.28am the gas was turned off and precisely at 6.30am 'A' Company was seen climbing out of the trenches and advancing. They were followed to time by 'B' Coy., 'C' Coy. moving forward from the support trenches at the same time. 'D' Company followed 'C' Coy at a distance of about 200 yards. The smoke cloud was dense, the sight was magnificent, the men were absolutely steely, moving forward in quick time exactly as if they were on parade. Owing to the density of the smoke cloud it was difficult to maintain direction, even the DOUBLE CRASSIER being almost completely obscured, the direction however was fairly maintained but a company of the Battalion to our right inclined too much to its left and overlapped our right.

Even though the smoke obscured the 1/6th until the last minute, the enemy reacted quickly. Despite four days of shelling the German shelters had remained undamaged and before long their machine-gun crews were in action. Undeterred by the gas cloud and the lines of men clambering through the broken wire, the men of the 22nd Reserve Infantry Regiment fought on until they were overrun:

> The four lines advanced in good order, all ranks behaving with the utmost steadiness in the face of a distinctive rifle and machine-gun fire in addition to the artillery barrage which was now intense. The wire was found to be very well cut in places, but there were considerable portions untouched and these formed a most formidable obstacle and caused considerable loss to the assaulting troops.

> The German machine-guns were in operation up to the last, the gunner on our front being bayoneted at his gun. The enemies troops maintained the fight until the leading company reached the top of the front trench when a considerable number retreated through the communications trench and across country, being lost to view in the smoke.

Now the battalion bombers, ten to a company, began searching out dugouts, forcing their occupants to surrender. In many cases their bombs failed to ignite, either soaked by the damp conditions or smothered in mud. Undeterred, they used their cudgels and daggers

140 Brigade established a line across the valley, Chalk Pit Copse lines the horizon. IWM Q37567

and in some cases used captured German stick grenades. The haul of prisoners was unexpected:

> *Some two hundred unwounded officers and men surrendered and a number were killed and wounded. The Officer Commanding was wounded and taken prisoner.*

The advance continued unabated, as some advanced across the open, others made their way along the German trenches. Rifleman Challoner led the way forward, shooting and bayoneting Germans as he charged down the communications trench at the head of the battalion bombers. He received the DCM.

> *There was little opposition in the German second line which, although manned at the time, was not apparently completed as a fire trench although very heavily wired.*

Their task complete, the 1/6th London began consolidating their gains, and collecting both London and German wounded.

The advance of the 1/7th London on the right of the Brigade front started well. Although the Germans reacted quickly, the 'Shiny

Seventh' soon crossed No Man's Land.

> The men went over the trenches at 6.30am, A and B Coys leading, followed by C and D. All Coys reached their objectives. The casualties in officers was severe. The Battalion fought splendidly.

Yet again the artillery had found their mark, smashing the wire entanglement to pieces. On the left, 'B' Company pushed forward along the foot of the Double Crassier alongside the 1/6th London. In a letter home, Private W E Morley described the advance:

> We went over the top into a perfect hail of machine-gun bullets - they let us have it properly; still we kept on and soon reached the German trenches. Most Germans turned tail and bolted, and we had some fine sport bringing them down. About four of us in five minutes turned about twenty out, eleven of them in one dugout. Another four, who held their arms above their heads, suddenly turned and bolted up the trench, so we let fly at them.

Major Bill Casson's 'A' Company advanced up the steep slopes of the Double Crassier in four waves. Despite fierce opposition, the Germans were quickly overwhelmed, and for the time being it seemed as though the slagheap had been secured. The Germans had other ideas, reserves were moved up, assembling out of sight at the foot of the heap. As Casson's men dug in, a determined counter-attack around the end of the slagheap threatened to drive them from their lofty perch. Major Casson immediately led his men against the threat, but when he was killed it seemed as though the City Battalion would be driven off the summit. Prompt action by CSM George Hill rallied the men and with bomb and bayonet, the Double Crassier was secured. Even so casualties had been heavy, and two companies from the 1/8th (Post Office Rifles) were sent forward by Brigade headquarters to secure the

The Double Crassier, Major Casson's men secured the slagheap on the left. IWM - Q37910

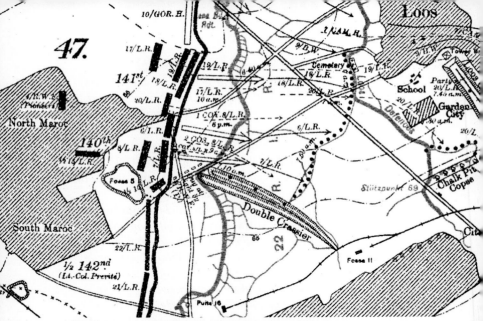

Map 19. Summary of 47th Division's advance across the Loos valley.

flank. The battalion bombers, led by Sergeant Thomas, were kept busy ferrying boxes of grenades up the to the top of the slagheap.

Late in the afternoon, as heavy rain fell, the padre buried eighty-seven officers and men of the battalion together at the foot of the Double Crassier. A Company's commander was among them:

> *Bill Casson's only thought was for the regiment and for the well being of his men. He was a perfect type of Regimental Officer, absolutely selfless, untiring, utterly loyal and completely fearless in battle, with an acute sense of humour and enjoyment of the simple things in life which made him the vast number of friends who felt that his death left a gap impossible to fill.*

The capture of the Double Crassier was seized upon by the London press, for it was the first time that one of their city's divisions had been seriously engaged. For weeks after the battle was known across the capital as "The Slag Heap Victory".

To the south of the Double Crassier, 142 Brigade carried out a Chinese attack. Dozens of wooden dummies, shaped and painted to look like prone figures, were made by the divisional carpenters and placed in No Man's Land. At zero hour strings pulled the figures up while the men of the 1/21st and 1/22nd London cheered and raised their bayonets over the parapet. The deception worked, for many of the dummies were found to have been peppered with bullets. It was one of the earliest attempts to deceive the Germans in such a manner, and its success led to the method being used on many occasions later in the war.

88

Chapter Seven

THE BATTLE CONTINUES

Deadlock at Lone Tree

By 9.00am Major-General Holland was in a predicament; although 1 Brigade had reached the outskirts of Hulluch, elsewhere the attack had broken down. To make matters worse, the two reserve companies of 157th Regiment had moved forward along Loos North Avenue, swelling the force opposite 2 Brigade to over 600 men. These reinforcements began to re-occupy the trenches about Bois Carré, effectively cutting off 1 Brigade. To counter this, Brigadier-General

Map 20. Situation on IV Corps front at noon.

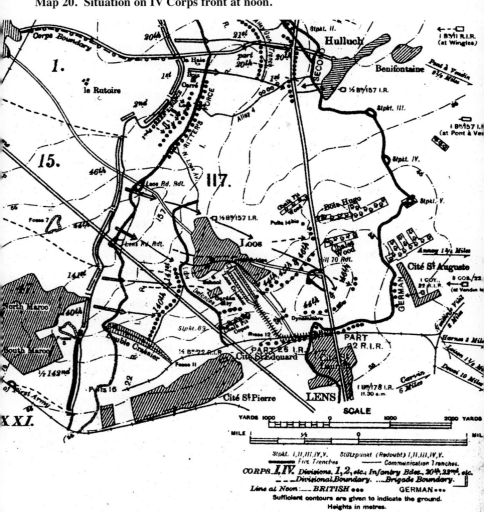

Reddie was forced to re-direct the 1st Black Watch to check the German move. Lieutenant-Colonel J Hamilton ordered 'B' Company forward first; the Highlanders were met by such a heavy fire that only thirty survived. The small group did, however, manage to thwart the German plan. In view of the casualties suffered, Hamilton decided against sending the rest of his battalion forward. Attempts to move north along the trenches to circumnavigate the German positions failed, for even now the communication trenches were still blocked.

At 10.00am the leading battalion of 3 Brigade was ordered forward; Brigadier-General Davies' report describes the brigade's dispositions about thirty minutes later:

> Munsters have been ordered to advance north of Bois Carré, and when through German trenches to wheel half right and attack in support of 1st Brigade. Welch follow in support, with orders to push through southern end of Hulluch. South Wales Borderers will be ready to support Welch.

Yet again the crowded trenches thwarted all attempts to move forward, and in frustration the Munsters (only 250 strong due to lack of reinforcements) were ordered to advance over the top. As the first company emerged from the trenches, Major Gorham instructed them to proceed to Bois Carré. However, by the time the order reached 'A' Company at the rear, the Germans had seen the tempting target. Major John Considine calmly organised his men as bullets began to find their mark. Seeing the huge numbers of men pinned down around Lone Tree, he decided to ignore his orders. Instead he ordered Second Lieutenant B D Conran to lead 'A' Company towards 2 Brigade. The regimental history explains what Major Considine was hoping to achieve:

> It was not his allotted task, and his orders were clear. A smaller man would have carried out his instructions to a letter. But not so Major Considine. He saw that if the enemy held this sector it would endanger the flanks of our successful attacks in the neighbouring sectors.

Part of 'B' Company followed, as did two platoons of 'D' Company under Lieutenant Richard Gethin. Advancing by platoon rushes, the Munsters moved south, crossing No Man's Land near Lone Tree. Wounded men cheered Considine's party forward as they passed. Considine was shot dead near the German wire, at the head of his men. His sergeant-major, CSM James Leahy, was killed as he rushed to his officer's aid. The brave attempt had done nothing to break the deadlock.

Meanwhile, Green's Force was still waiting for instructions. Major-General Holland's order to attack had been sent at 9.10am. However, three runners had died trying to reach the front line, and it took nearly two hours to get the message to Colonel Green. Another hour passed before the London Scottish and the 1/9th King's (Liverpool) were ready to move. Major Lindsay wanted to take his men north to outflank the Germans, but Colonel Green refused, having decided that the order had to be obeyed literally. Around midday two companies of each battalion began to move forward. By moving forward in short rushes, half a company at a time, casualties were kept to a minimum. It was a brave attempt, but it made no difference to the situation because the belt of wire was still intact. Many were shot down as they tried to cut a way through. The survivors formed a firing line close to the wire, making cover with their entrenching tools. One of the 1/9th King's machine-guns was brought across No Man's Land under a hail of bullets, and used to provide covering fire.

After six hours of deadlock, Major-General Holland decided to abandon further frontal assaults. Instead his troops would outflank the Lone Tree position and the order to 2 Brigade explains his intentions:

> *Collect all available men of your brigade, leaving only sufficient to hold the line. Move them down to the Vermelles - Loos Road and across the German trenches at the Loos Road Redoubt. Then wheel up to your left and attack along line North Loos Avenue and Loos - La Bassée road, so as to get behind the*

German machine-gun team's view of No Man's Land. IWM - Q28976

Germans holding up your brigade.

The Divisional reserve, the 1st Gloucesters, were detailed to assist the stricken brigade. At the front line Colonel Green ordered one company of the London Scottish to make a flank attack from the north.

However, before these outflanking moves developed, assistance came from an unexpected quarter. The 2nd Welch, led by Lieutenant-Colonel A G Prothero, had set off from Le Rutoire at 12.30pm in support of the 2nd Munsters:

> *We moved off in extended order two companies leading and two behind, fully imagining that the MUNSTERS' were in front. We came under heavy fire immediately from the Germans who were by the BOIS CARRE but they did no damage. We then crossed over the German first and second lines, not losing anyone.*

As Prothero's men advanced over the top of the ridge they came under heavy fire from Hulluch, losing 150 men in a short space of time. By the time he reached Gun Trench, Lieutenant-Colonel Prothero was convinced that the Royal Munsters had become lost. To move forward would result in heavy casualties. In an attempt to find a safer route forward Prothero ordered the battalion to wheel right in the hope of bypassing Hulluch. By chance this movement brought the Welch behind Captain Ritter's position. Responding to this new threat the Germans manned the reverse side of their support trench. Surrounded and with ammunition running out, the men of 157th Regiment began to surrender. Those facing the Welch surrendered first, as the war diary reports:

> *Suddenly the fire from our right slackened and it at last stopped altogether and a German bearing a white flag came towards us. He was sent by the Germans holding out to arrange their surrender. We then captured 160 men and five officers.*

The remainder of the Germans, over 400, led by Captain Ritter, capitulated soon afterwards. A Stuart Dolden describes the moment of surrender in his autobiography *Cannon Fodder*:

> *At one moment there was an intense and nerve shattering struggle with death screaming*

through the air. Then, as if with the wave of a magic wand, all was changed; all over No Man's Land troops came out of their trenches, or rose from where the ground where they had been lying. Prisoners were everywhere.

For eight hours 600 men had held up ten times their number, inflicting over 2,500 casualties. 157th Regiment's war diary modestly describes the exploits of its 1st Battalion;

> *...repulsed the constant British attacks, but no reinforcements could be sent forward to it from Hulluch throughout the morning in answer to Captain Ritter's requests. At length, the battalion ran out of ammunition and hand grenades, so that, when strong British forces began to move west of Hulluch across the rear of its position, it had to surrender.*

After collecting their weapons, Ritter's men were led back to Le Rutoire Farm under escort.

It was now past 3.00pm and, with darkness approaching, Brigadier-General Pollard and Colonel Green assembled their depleted commands, numbering only a quarter of their strength. As rain clouds gathered the men moved over the Grenay Ridge, leaving behind the ghastly scenes around Lone Tree. In front, 2,000 metres away, they could see the Lens highway running across the valley. To their right was the village of Loos and Tower Bridge, burning in the gathering darkness. Ahead were their objectives, Bois Hugo and the chimney that stood beside Puits 14 bis.

The valley was unusually quiet, the fighting having subsided with both sides digging in ready for morning. By dusk the western end of

Desolation after the battle. Q 28967

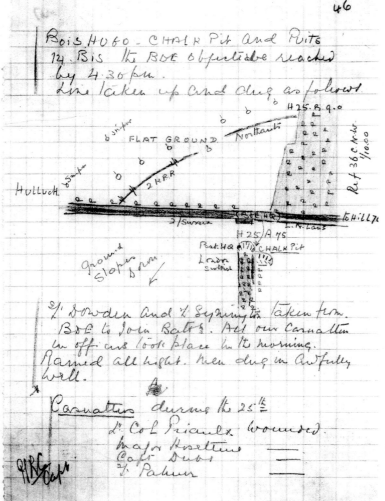

Bois HUGO - CHALK PIT and PITS
14. Bis the BOE objectibe reached
by 4.30 pm.
Line taken up and dug as follows

FLAT GROUND

Hulluch

2 H.R.R.

Northants

H 25. B. 9. 0

Ref 36 c.N.w. 1/10000

2/Sussex

Bn HQ

L.N.Laus

H 25/A 75

Bat.HQ

CHALK PIT

London Scottish

Hill 7

ground slopes from

H 25/A 75

2/ Dowden and 2/ Symington taken from.
BoE to join Bat⁸. All our casualties
in officers took place in the morning.
Rained all night. Men dug in awfully
well.

Casualties during the 25th
L. Col. Pricaulx wounded.
Major Roseltine
Capt Dubs
2/ Palmer

Map 21. Sketch map of 2 Brigade's overnight positions north of Bois Hugo.

Bois Hugo had been secured, and the Scots in Chalet Wood were relieved to find British troops to their left. Entrenching in the hard ground, 2 Brigade established a line on the flat ground north of the wood, while Green's force provided support in the Chalk Pit.

1 Brigade waits for reinforcements at Hulluch

During all this time the three battalions of 1 Brigade, or what was left of them, waited patiently in front of Hulluch. For seven hours they saw no-one except advanced parties of the 7th Division to their right.

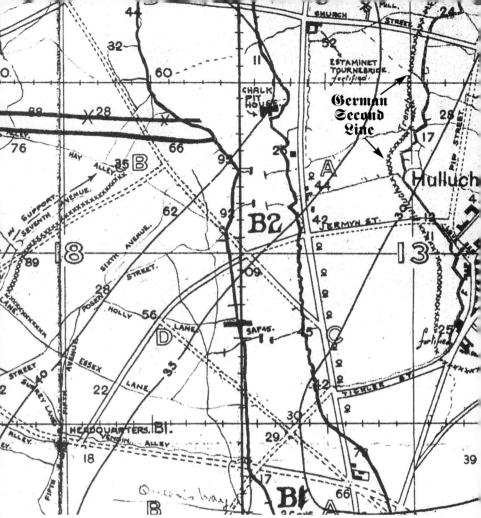

Map 22 Trench map of the area west of Hulluch after the battle, the defence line protecting the village is clearly shown.

It seemed as though the battlefield was deserted. Around noon what was left of the 2nd Royal Munsters, about one hundred men, arrived. Unfortunately, they were too few and it was too late. For over five hours there had been a considerable breach in the German line, with no formed German resistance to prevent a breakthrough. With reinforcements 1 Brigade could have broken through, as the Cameron Highlanders' diary reports:

> There undoubtedly was, for an appreciable period, a gap in the enemy's defences, but the necessary troops to force their way through were not at hand.

Instead 1 Brigade was forced onto the defensive. The Camerons in Hulluch were compelled to make a hasty retreat when the reserve battalion of the 157th Regiment arrived shortly after noon. Three hours later they attacked from the village, driving 1 Brigade's outposts across the Lens road. Although they were outnumbered and isolated, Reddie's brigade easily saw off the attack. Shortly afterwards, substantial reinforcements arrived, the 2nd Welch and the 1st South Wales Borderers of 3 Brigade. It was, however, too late to attack Hulluch. With nightfall approaching General Reddie instructed his men to dig in along Alley 4, a communications trench west of the road.

Just before midnight a second counter-attack struck. Lieutenant C Gentry-Birch, one of only two surviving officers of the 8th Berkshires, describes how his men fought almost to the last man:

> *At 11.30pm the Germans counter-attacked in large numbers, driving in our right flank. We retired to the position we had held in the afternoon. The Germans continued to push the counter-attack. Our support line then opened fire and we were caught between the two fires. We then made our way as well as possible to our supporting line. Only six of the Berkshires returned safely. The Germans continued to push the counter-attack, but suffered heavily and were driven back.*

Meanwhile, the South Wales Borderers, with their considerable experience, managed to foil the German attack with light casualties. As the Germans approached they attempted to fool Lieutenant Colonel Gwynn's men with shouts of "Don't shoot" and "We are the Welsh". Realising the ruse, the Borderers opened fire at point blank range. The following morning nearly every man possessed a prized German helmet.

What were needed were substantial reserves to take advantage of the breakthrough. The day's fighting had exhausted Major-General Holland's Division, and although they had broken the German first line they were too weak to hold their positions. Nightfall found 1 Brigade and 3 Brigade facing Hulluch. Neither Brigadier-General Reddie nor Brigadier-General Davies knew of the whereabouts of 2 Brigade and it was not until after midnight that scouts from the two halves of the Division met. A gap of 1,200 metres between the two commands was devoid of troops, and General Holland had nothing to fill it with. All he could do was wait for the arrival of the reserve, 21st and 24th Divisions of IX Corps.

Chapter Eight

THE BATTLE FOR HILL 70

By 10.30am 15th Division had reached its high water mark. The majority of 46 and 44 Brigades were scattered across the eastern and southern slopes of Hill 70, pinned down close to the German wire. Without substantial reserves the attack was doomed. Meanwhile, Lieutenant-Colonel Sandilands (minus his battalion) found two companies of the 7th Royal Scots Fusiliers waiting for orders. Sensing that all was not well at the front, he led them out of the ruins and up the hill:

> On arrival about half-way up the slope of Hill 70 I heard that a body of two or three hundred of the Brigade, including many of my own men, had pushed on too quickly, down the further slope of Hill 70, where they were encountering the most serious resistance from the Germans around SAINT LAURENT, and could not get any further. I proceeded further up the slope and getting reports that the position already referred to was becoming untenable decided to dig in at once with what troops I had on the reverse slope.

Lieutenant-Colonel Lloyd, 9th Black Watch, had already gone forward to the right flank, having received reports that his men had been unable to contact 47th (London) Division on Loos Crassier. As senior officer on the hill, Colonel Sandilands assessed the situation. To the south and east the unbroken wire covering Cité St Laurent and Cité St Auguste blocked the way forward. It was also obvious that the men near to the

The slope beyond Loos leading up to the summit of Hill 70. IWM - Q43112

wire were under heavy fire. To the north there was no sign of 1st Division crossing the Loos valley. To safeguard Hill 70 from counter-attack Major-General McCracken's orders called for:

A sufficient force to consolidate and hold it until troops from the divisional reserve can be pushed up to take it over...the senior commanding officer on the spot will issue necessary orders for consolidating that position against possible attack from direction of Lens.

With the assistance of Lieutenant-Colonel Wallace, the 10th Gordons' commanding officer, Sandilands set about establishing a firing line on the summit of the hill. Realising that they had little time to spare, Lieutenant Colonel Sandilands decided against trying to fortify the redoubt. Instead the men were ordered to dig in west of the redoubt, where a natural earth bank provided cover. Eventually about 400 men were gathered together, including the two companies of Scots Fusiliers. Sandiland's report explains the situation on the hill:

There was very heavy firing in front: the few officers and men returning all stated that the line in front had been practically wiped out, this influenced me further to hold on to the back line at all costs. From now on the mixture of units made Command most difficult...I would like to mention here that Colonel Wallace of the 10th Gordons rendered me great assistance in keeping the mixed units together and the Scots Fusiliers stuck to most staunchly and were in a great measure responsible for the hill being held. Finally the line settled down and became quite confident.

Lieutenant-Colonel Sandilands would have been proud to see his battalion flag, a yellow signalling flag with a piece of Cameron tartan sewn onto it, flying proudly above the redoubt.

At the front line, the situation was quickly deteriorating. Numerous requests for artillery support were misunderstood. The heavy artillery was ordered to concentrate its fire on Cité St Auguste, leaving the troops in front of Cité St. Laurent unsupported. At Corps headquarters it appeared that the advance was going well and just before 11.00am General Rawlinson ordered McCracken to send 45 Brigade forward though Cité St Auguste.

In actual fact the Scots were near breaking point. German reinforcements had begun to arrive and around midday counter-attacked the right of the line near Loos Crassier. The debriefing report of the 10th Gordon Highlanders describes how the men tried to call for assistance:

Lieutenant Robinson was the only officer left. The party was about 600 strong of different regiments. Various attempts were made to communicate back. Sergt. Aitkin and Pte. McKeller crawled back and the former reached O.C. 7th Camerons who was digging in on the reserve slope of Hill 70. Pte Davidson also went back with a message...

With the full facts at hand, Lieutenant Colonel Sandilands decided against sending reinforcements forward. Instead he took steps to recall the forward line from its exposed position to strengthen the hill top. When fresh reinforcements arrived they could renew the attack. Sandilands' main problem was how to communicate the message.

Eventually the Germans provided the solution. A counter-attack from the Dynamitière, an explosives store on the northern outskirts of Cité St Laurent, began to exploit the Scots exposed right flank. Unsupported and outflanked they began to retire. On the summit of the hill, Scout-Sergeant Thomas Lamb grabbed the battalion flag and began waving it, acting as a rallying point. Seeing this as sign of weakness, the Germans around the Dynamitière began moving forward through gaps in their wire. Their cheers inspired their comrades further east to charge forward. Some of the Scots ran back up the slope, others were captured or killed and only fifty were taken unwounded. The war diary of the 178th Regiment proudly describes its counter-attack:

Map 23. The battle for Hill 70, the Scots are forced to retire from the redoubt.

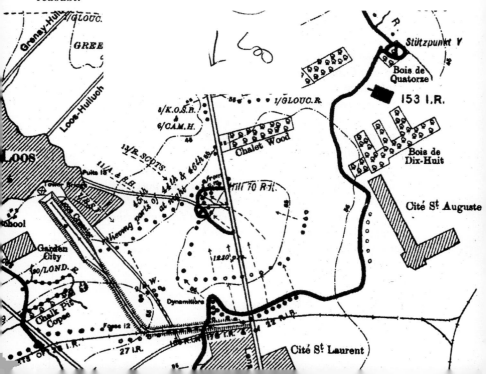

To those who took part, this charge up the slope of Hill 70 will be an unforgettable experience, whilst to those who watched it gave a war picture such as will seldom recur. On reaching the summit, Adjutant Ryssel was mortally wounded by a shell splinter, shouting as he lay dying, 'We have it, hurrah!'

Captain Strang, the only unhurt officer of the 8th Seaforths watched the situation deteriorate from the top of the hill. His report describes how the perseverance of one young officer prevented the Scots from being swept off the hill:

I had retired to the top of the hill to attempt an appreciation of the situation and I got to the Keep found there a young engineer, Lt. Johnson, who instantly convinced me of the necessity of rallying the men there and holding the hill on this line. We failed to induce the men to remain in the Keep, but succeeded in making them hold onto a bank on which the whole line subsequently retired, and getting fire under control we were able to hold up the German counter-attack. It certainly looked for the moment as if the whole offensive was going to be swept off the hill, and I think it was due entirely to the judgement of the young Engineer Officer that the situation was saved.

Although the engineers had been sent forward with orders to consolidate the captured hill, Captain Cardew led No. 3 and No. 4 sections of 73rd Company RE into the firing line. The Company war diary relates how the engineers counter-attacked:

...they reached the crest of the hill and saw some infantry in the keep hard pressed. The R.E. then advanced to the keep and tried to hold it. All had however to retire, as the machine-gun fire was so hot. They went back behind the ridge and started to dig in; but Capt. Cardew decided to have another go at the keep and advanced again with R.E. only after he and Lieut. Johnson had got themselves a machine-gun into position. They advanced to the keep and Captain Cardew, Lieut. Johnson and about 16 R.E. got in, but had to come out again. At this point Capt. Cardew was wounded seriously and Lieut. Johnson was wounded in the leg.

Lieutenant Frederick Johnson, an engineering student who had volunteered in August 1914, stuck to his post until relieved at midnight. As his unit war diary mentions he had:

...rallied his men and the parties of infantry without officers, and showed great coolness and gallantry.

Lieutenant Johnson was awarded the Victoria Cross and quickly rose to the rank of Major. During the Battle of Cambrai he was mortally wounded, succumbing to his injuries on 11 December 1917. His name is engraved on the Cambrai Memorial to the Missing.

German counter-attacks persisted into the afternoon, and with no reinforcements to hand, Sandilands' men were hard pressed to hold onto the crest line. The 7th Royal Scots Fusilers were already in the thick of the fighting on top of the hill. A second battalion of 45 Brigade, the 6th Cameron Highlanders, was holding a defensive flank near Chalet Wood. Meanwhile, the 11th Argylls and 13th Royal Scots had still not reached Loos.

Second Lieutenant Frederick Johnson VC.

With the summit of the hill in German hands, their batteries could shell the valley at will, making it impossible to bring artillery forward to support further attacks. Major-General McCracken knew that he could ask no more from his men. He was, however, proud of his Division's achievements. In four hours the Scots had advanced over two miles, storming a succession of strongly held positions along the way. Lord Kitchener could be confident that, given the right circumstances, his New Armies were capable of beating the Germans.

A mixed group of walking wounded await evacuation.

Chapter Nine

IX CORPS – THE RESERVE

The deployment of the reserves during the Battle of Loos was (and still is) an area of controversy. Field Marshal Sir John French and General Sir Douglas Haig did not see eye to eye on the positioning of the reserves, even more so when the battle was over. The political manoeuvring that went on during the early winter ended in the replacement of French by Haig. Although this is not the place for studying the arguments, the condition and treatment of the reserves is

Troops making their way past buses that had, the previous year, transported men of the Royal Naval Division. Note the 'R.N.D.' on the bus fronts. The Royal Naval Division was serving in Gallipoli at the time of Loos. IWM - Q60740

relevant to the development of the battle.

All along IV Corps front small parties of men were facing the German Second Line. With nightfall approaching reserves were needed to punch a way through to the open countryside. First Army intended to use the 21st and the 24th Divisions on the 26th, attacking the German line between Hulluch and Hill 70. They were, however, having difficulties of their own.

The arrival of 62 Brigade

By late morning the situation on IV Corps front was promising. In places, on the left of 1st Division sector and on 15th Division's front, clean breakthroughs had been made. What was clear, though, was the

fact that heavy casualties had reduced the advance parties to a mere skeleton of their paper strength. On the right, 47th Division had secured its objectives without committing its reserve brigade, and for the time being the corps flank was safe. The only failure had been on the right of 1st Division at Lone Tree. Even so, Major-General Holland was in the process of reinforcing the sector in the hope of bludgeoning a way through.

Lieutenant-General Rawlinson's main area of concern was Hill 70, where the Scots were engaged in a running battle for the redoubt. Messages from the front line reported heavy casualties, wavering morale and German counter-attacks. If the hill fell into German hands the chances of following up the early success would diminish rapidly. Having no reserves of its own, IV Corps needed assistance from First Army reserves and General Haig released a single brigade to aid the Scots. It was 62 Brigade, from Major-General C W Jacob's 21st Division. The lead brigade of the 24th Division, the 73rd, was also ordered forward to reinforce I Corps.

At midday Brigadier-General Ernest Wilkinson was instructed to advance to the map reference for Hill 70. In the knowledge that the situation east of Loos could change at any moment his orders were, to put it mildly, vague. As the men ate their dinners, Wilkinson's battalion commanders gathered around their leader's map. Their instructions were brief:

> ...We do not know what has happened on Hill 70. You must go and find out: if the Germans hold it, attack them; if our people are there, support them; if no one is there, dig in.

Around 3.00pm the two leading battalions marched out of Mazingarbe village, heading along the Lens road. Almost at once they were stopped by a military policeman, who ordered them to proceed in open formation as they were about to enter the 'battle zone'. Experienced

officers would have ignored the instruction, but those of the 8th East Yorkshires and the 10th Green Howards knew no different. The columns reorganised and continued, their progress hampered by the swarms of wounded and gassed men hobbling in the opposite direction.

With the sights and sounds of battle numbing their senses, the leading sections reached the old front line, near Dud Corner, at 4.30pm. The marching formation, column of fours with platoons at 100 metre intervals, was entirely inappropriate for the conditions. Lieutenant-Colonels Way and Hadow led their heavily laden troops down the Lens road towards the burning ruins, ignorant of the fact that their movement was being watched. German artillery crews across the valley in Cité St Pierre could hardly believe their luck. Shrapnel soon began to shower the column and many were hit before they could take cover. The brigade transport, which was still accompanying the men, was unable to escape. Shells destroyed the convoy and the tangle of wrecked carts and dead animals blocked the road for a number of days. Reforming cautiously, the two battalions pushed on looking for Hill 70. Without guides or detailed maps to direct them the Yorkshiremen advanced across country heading for the high ground they believed to be Hill 70.

Before long they came across Lieutenant-Colonel Hubback's 1/20th London Battalion, which was holding a communications trench to the north of Chalk Pit Copse. The St Pancras men watched in dismay as the two battalions casually went forwards towards the enemy occupied copse. Lieutenant-Colonel Hubbuck tried to stop the impending disaster:

> *About 5.00pm... the 8th Bn. EAST YORKSHIRE REGT. and 10th Bn. YORKSHIRE REGT. came through the line we were*

Brigade's transport lies wrecked on the Grenay Ridge. IWM Q28971

holding. I was able to stop some of the senior officers and ask them where they were going. I was told that they had been told to take LOOS and occupy HILL 70; they appeared to have no definite orders or any idea as to the direction of HILL 70. I told a senior officer of the 8th EAST YORKS. (I think the C.O.) the direction of HILL 70 and also that LOOS had been occupied by the 47th Division since that morning...

From what I can gather from the officers the orders they had received were most indefinite, they appeared to have no maps and certainly no idea of localities.

Despite Hubback's remonstrations, the East Yorkshires and the two leading companies of the Green Howards marched blindly forward up the slope. As they approached Chalk Pit Copse heavy machine-gun fire opened up, sending the Yorkshiremen reeling back towards the London held trench. The disaster was compounded when the rear companies of the Green Howards, who were waiting in reserve at the foot of the hill, saw the survivors falling back. In the failing light, they mistook their comrades for Germans, and opened fire. For a time Lieutenant-Colonels' Hadow and Way were powerless to stop their men from killing each other. As darkness fell order was finally restored and the battalions reformed.

Lieutenant-Colonel Way led two of his companies back up the hill so they could reinforce the 1/20th London's line, the rest of his men joined in the house clearing operations. Meanwhile, the Green Howards anxiously waited in reserve near the village cemetery. Although the line had been stabilised, a message from the East

Map 24. German trenches north of Double Crassier, Welwyn Garden City and the Chalk Pit are to the south of Loos Crassier.

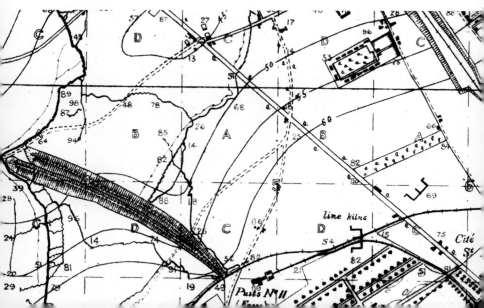

Yorkshires illustrates how precarious it was:

> *Enemy shelling PYLONS and good number of machine-guns and snipers worrying us. Machine guns are said to be in wood R of our own front – about E* [this was Chalk Pit Copse]. *Unless artillery help us we shall suffer from heavy gun fire. Can artillery engage enemy's artillery and keep down fire. Our own forward positions are at the outside 800 yards in front of LOOS PYLONS. Have not enough men to hold position if attacked at daylight.*

It is now time to turn our attentions to the rest of the brigade, the 12th and 13th Northumberland Fusiliers. The two battalions left Mazingarbe about an hour after the Yorkshiremen. Apart from the usual struggle to make progress along the crowded roads, they managed to reach Loos without difficulty. Brigadier-General Wilkinson found to his dismay that the rest of his command had gone astray; with no time to search for them he reported to 45 Brigade's headquarters in the village square. Brigadier Wallerstein was able to tell him that the hill was held by his men; they were, however, exhausted and low on ammunition.

Initially two platoons of the 12th Northumberland Fusiliers made their way up the hill to make contact and establish a safe route forward. When two more platoons arrived, the 9th Black Watch and 10th Gordons assumed that their relief was underway. Lieutenant-Colonel Sandilands and Lieutenant-Colonel Wallace gratefully collected their fatigued men and led them down into the village. By 11.00pm there was a large hole in the front line, the misunderstanding had left the single company of Fusiliers in sole possession of Hill 70.

The final battalion in Wilkinson's command, the 13th Northumberland Fusiliers, was ordered to relieve 46 Brigade. Little had been heard of them since the morning, but it was believed that Brigadier-General Matheson's men held Chalet Wood. As the Fusiliers made there way through the ruined streets, they were fortunate to meet Lieutenant-Colonel Purvis, the senior surviving officer in charge of the Chalet Wood position. Purvis ordered three of the Fusilier companies to dig in on the lower slopes of the hill, to support his line. The remaining company was instructed to strengthen the Scots, by extending its line south of Chalet Wood. For a second time the arrival of a single company was mistaken for a full relief.

The attempt to strengthen 15th Division's front had failed miserably, and was a perfect example of how poor information and vague orders could lead to disaster. It would be several hours before the mistakes were rectified and for a time only two companies held the line between Chalet Wood and Hill 70. Luckily the Germans knew nothing of the situation for they too were exhausted by the day's fighting. They made only two counter-attacks and, as luck would have it, they fell on the strongest part of the line, near the end of Loos Crassier where the 7th Royal Scots Fusiliers were holding out. As dawn approached the reluctant Scots were led back up the hillside to their old positions, where they would have to fight again.

21st and 24th Divisions move onto the battlefield

As the afternoon wore on the men waiting in the villages to the rear grew restless, wondering when they would be called upon. As the hours passed the tension mounted, and men tried to find out information by whatever means available. The streets were bustling with transport, ambulances, supply wagons and carts of every description. There were also hundreds of wounded, limping along covered in chalky mud and bandages. Many were coughing and choking from the effects of the gas. Every now and again German prisoners passed by, and they were viewed with suspicion. For many of the New Army men the sights were disturbing, for they had never seen anything like it before.

As dusk approached, the rest of 21st and 24th Division brigades received orders to move out without delay. The experiences of 63 Brigade, 21st Division's leading brigade, illustrate the difficulties encountered by the reserves as they made their way forward. Reluctantly, the men formed up, they were tired and hungry, not having

The landscape begins to change as the troops approach the battlefield.

had any hot food as their cookers had failed to arrive. For three hours they marched along the Lens highway in the pouring rain. Near Fosse 7 Brigadier-General Norman Nickalls moved to the front of the column, leading the 8th Lincolns and the 8th Somerset Light Infantry across country by compass bearing. Meanwhile, the 12th West Yorkshires and the 10th York and Lancaster continued along the road as far as Lens Road Redoubt. The men were mesmerised by the scene, all around lines of gun batteries fired incessantly on invisible targets, while the skyline in front of them glowed orange. Second Lieutenant F Cragg of the Lincolns recorded his view of the panorama:

> As we got to the crest-line, now free from obstruction, we could see the countryside slightly, and what a sight met our eyes! Right ahead of us was Loos in flames, this was the glare that puzzled us; the twin towers of the mine standing out like great oil towers on a burning oil field.

As the Lincolnshire Regimental History explains, this stage of the advance was particularly difficult and the lack of information available to the brigade is astonishing:

> The Commanding Officer, Adjutant and Company Commanders were given a compass bearing to march on and by 11pm the Lincolnshire had cleared the last line of old German trenches. So far as we knew only open country lay before them. They then lay down for a considerable time, apparently to allow other troops to come up.

Brigadier-General Nickall's assembled his brigade on the slopes east of Loos Road Redoubt. Not surprisingly some troops became lost and Lieutenant-Colonel Denny leading the two support companies of the Somersets went astray. They never rejoined the brigade, and eventually attached themselves to the Scots on Hill 70.

> Confronted with a difficult situation on unknown ground, not having been in action before, without guidance from the Commanders and Staffs who had been in the sector and had studied its features for months past, it is not surprising that this night march was most trying to all ranks.

Meanwhile, 72 Brigade had been making its way forward from Beuvry, suffering the same sorts of delays on the way through Vermelles. Around midnight Brigadier-General Mitford's men began picking their way across the battlefield, stumbling and cursing as they made their way through the network of trenches. Shortly after 1.00am Brigadier-General Nickalls met Brigadier-General Mitford on the eastern slope of Grenay Ridge. In accordance with their instructions the two decided

109

to push on to the German Second Line.

During the afternoon First Army headquarters was forced to change its view on the progress of the battle. Although IV Corps had cleared the first line of defence, it had not broken through the second line. Heavy casualties meant that the three assault divisions could not be relied on to carry out offensive operations on the 26th. First Army intended to launch an attack the following morning and ordered IX Corps to halt its brigades on the Grenay Ridge, where they would wait for further instructions. General Mitford received the order in time, and was able to instruct his battalions to take cover in the German trenches. Meanwhile, 71 Brigade, following behind, occupied the assembly trenches near Lone Tree.

63 Brigade take over Bois Hugo

General Nickalls' instruction to halt on the Grenay Ridge failed to reach him and the brigade continued to move east, skirting the flaming ruins of Loos. As they crossed the valley, the brigade came under heavy machine-gun fire and for a time it appeared as though it was directed from Chalk Pit Wood. In fact the wood was held by Green's Force, who were in support of 2 Brigade in Bois Hugo. The war diary of 63 Brigade reports how luck prevented a catastrophe:

No information had been received that the position of the Chalk Pit was in occupation of our troops. Luckily no unfortunate results took place, which might very easily have occurred with new troops advancing to a position at night which was not known to be in our possession. It reflects great credit on the officers concerned, who kept their men so well in hand...The absence of information of what was happening elsewhere was nothing short of disastrous, as no one knew what anyone else was doing.

The fire actually came from Hill 70, where the Germans were engaged with the Northumberland Fusiliers and Scots on the summit.

With a disaster averted, Brigadier-General Nickalls sought out Brigadier-General Pollard. The two eventually met in the Chalk Pit and came to the decision that 63 Brigade would relief 2 Brigade. Throughout the remaining hours of darkness the New Army men took over the shallow trenches in and around Bois Hugo. Although they were tired, having spent the last eight hours on the march, there was no time to rest. With dawn approaching, the men tried to dig into the hard chalk with their entrenching tools. Brigadier-General Nickalls knew that his brigade now held the front line. Not sure of where troops were on his flanks, he planned to wait until further orders arrived. The

Brigade was deployed as follows:

A, B and C companies of the Lincolnshire held an east to west line, east of the Lens-Hulluch road and along the southern edge of Bois Hugo and facing Hill 70; three companies of the West Yorks were on the left of the Lincolnshire facing east; the fourth company (D) of the Lincolnshire, with the remaining company of the West Yorks were in reserve in the angle formed by the front line; the Somersets (less two companies) were between the western side of the Lens-Hulluch road and the Chalk Pit Wood, while the York and Lancaster, who by this time had joined, carried the Brigade line along the road north of the Chalk Pit; but the left flank was entirely in the air!

64 Brigade advances onto the battlefield

Brigadier-General Gerald Gloster's brigade followed 63 Brigade along the Bethune-Lens Road as the sky grew dark. Almost at once traffic congestion at Mazingarbe delayed the brigade by over an hour. Soaked by the pouring rain, the men marched along the dark cobbled road as far as Philosophe. Here Gloster deployed his brigade south of the road on a two battalion frontage. The companies formed up in columns of four at ten paces interval, a line of scouts covered the line of the march. The Brigade diary describes the difficulties encountered in deploying:

It took three hours to issue orders; unload machine-guns, ammunition, bombs and tools for manhandling; marshal and separate transport; and to form up the Brigade. Any reconnaissance of our line of march was impossible, but it was decided to move on a compass bearing.

Moving east, the troops picked their way across the battlefield, ahead Tower Bridge, silhouetted by fire, dominated the night sky. Crossing the old front line near Loos Road Redoubt, the men, encumbered by full packs, struggled in and out of the battered trenches.

At 1.00am we found ourselves crossing the British front system of trenches. Some trenches could be jumped, some had had narrow causeways filled in across them, across others we

Loos colliery towers over the desolate countryside.

*found planks. But the crossing was interminable, each trench
necessitating a halt to let units file over and then reform the
Brigade beyond. While crossing both systems we were
spasmodically shelled, and the shells seemed to follow us up,
though luckily those that fell nearest were blind. We attributed
this shelling later to two German spies who were found next day
left behind in their trenches and working a telephone. They were
found and shot by the Guards Division.*

Eventually after an eight hour march Brigadier-General Gloster called
a halt north of the burning houses of Loos. Patrols were sent forward
to contact 63 Brigade, but returned without finding them. As the
Brigade war diary reports, Gloster was faced with a dilemma:

*Daylight was now rapidly approaching. It was possible that
the 63 Inf Bde had mistaken its direction and there was nothing
between us and the enemy. If this were so, it was now too late to
push on to the LENS-HULLUCH road as there was not enough
darkness left in which to consolidate it, and the risk of moving
forward on unknown ground and stumbling on the enemy without
having touch with any neighbouring troops, or being caught by
him in open coverless ground at daylight in an isolated situation
was too great. On the other hand if the 63 Inf Bde were ahead
and had consolidated themselves on the LENS-HULLUCH road
as directed, we had reached just the right position in their rear
from which to support them.*

General Gloster rightly assumed that Nickalls Brigade was just in front
and opted to deploy north of Loos. German communication trenches
were used to provide cover wherever possible. The 14th and 15th
Durham Light Infantry were in front lined out alongside the Grenay-
Hulluch road; five hundred metres in support were the 9th and 10th
KOYLIs along the Loos-Haisnes road.

Changing circumstances, poor planning and a complete lack of staff
work had scattered First Army's reserve across the battlefield, In many
cases corps and divisional headquarters did not know where their
troops were. One brigade, the 62nd had been fragmented and engaged
on Hill 70. A second, 73 Brigade, had been despatched to I Corps to
help shore up the front at Fosse 8. The remaining brigades had spent a
miserable night, marching for hours along dark, wet streets before they
reached the battlefield. 24th Division's two remaining brigades
sheltering in trenches on the Grenay Ridge, were well placed for the
planned attack in the morning.

Chapter Ten

26 SEPTEMBER, EARLY DEVELOPMENTS

15th Division attempts to capture Hill 70

The first glimmer of daylight found Brigadier General Francis Wallerstein's 45 Brigade in a precarious position on Hill 70. German troops still occupied the redoubt and its outlying trench. Meanwhile, Wallerstein's men held a series of shallow trenches arrayed in a semi-circle opposite the redoubt. On the left 'B' company of the 13th Royal Scots, supported by a company of the 7th Royal Scots Fusiliers, were in a perilous position. At first light enfilade fire from the direction of Chalet Wood swept their position, killing their commanding officer, Captain Bethune Bruce. The centre of the line was held by the 11th Argyll and Sutherland Highlanders, they reported that:

> *The morning was spent in close touch with the enemy, the near face of the HILL being continuously swept by enemy machine-gun fire and high explosive shell. 45th Brigade's right flank was held by the 7th Scots Fusiliers.*

First Army headquarters intended to attack the German Second Line between Hulluch and Cité St Auguste at 11.00am. They did, however, recognise that the redoubt on the summit of Hill 70 could enfilade the assault troops. Rawlinson instructed McCracken's Division to clear the hill at 9.00am, Brigadier-General Wilkinson's 62 Brigade would support the hard-pressed Scots. However, only two of Wilkinson's battalions were in a position to attack the hill, the remainder had already been engaged elsewhere.

When the orders arrived in the early hours Brigadiers Wallerstein and Wilkinson met to discuss its practicalities:

> *45th and 62nd Brigades will attack Hill 70 at 9.00am today. 45th Brigade will attack from the west with its left on the track from Loos through the Hill 70 Redoubt to the Lens - La Bassée road. The 62nd Brigade will attack from the north-west with its right on the same track. The attack will be preceded by an hour's intense bombardment by all available guns, and artillery barrages will be established on the enemy's trenches south and east of Hill 70 during and after the attack .... Before the bombardment of the Hill 70 Redoubt begins the infantry will be withdrawn to a safe distance.*

The two men recognised the difficulties of complying with the instructions. With time running short, it would be too dangerous to attempt to reorganise the front with the Germans in close proximity. Instead the Scots would attack the summit from their existing positions. The Royal Scots would attack the north face of the redoubt and beyond. In the centre the 11th Argylls would take the keep, while the 7th Royal Scots Fusiliers assaulted the south face. Brigadier Wilkinson's two available battalions, the 10th Green Howards and the 12th Northumberland Fusiliers, would be in support, advancing from their positions east of Loos. At 6.45am Brigadier-General Wallerstein summoned his battalion COs to issue instructions, as recorded in the Argylls' war diary;

> *To withdraw under cover of a heavy bombardment of HILL 70, which was to commence at 8am and last until 9am, endeavour to reorganise and along with 13th Royal Scots and 7th Royal Scots Fusiliers deliver a simultaneous assault on Hill 70 at 9am.*

Meanwhile, the artillery officers were finding it difficult to comply with their orders at such short notice. A number of field batteries had collected in the valley overnight. They had little time to locate their positions and register their guns. The Scots marked their front line with flags, but their efforts were in vain. A thick mist obscured the hilltop, forcing the gunners to fire blind. The heavy artillery had to remain in

An artillery man's view of Hill 70, looking across the northern outskirts of Loos. IWM - Q43111

their original positions, firing at long range, due to the short notice.

As 8.00am approached 45 Brigade was hurriedly trying to withdraw its men. In many instances the message did not arrive before the artillery opened fire. The war diary of the 13th Royal Scots illustrates the bitterness exhibited by some:

> *At the time fixed for the assault the Regt. to advance in lines of 2 platoons order of Co's. A, B, C, D, MG; D Coy to bring up entrenching tools and entrench the position. The time at our disposal for issuing orders and forming and direct detailed scheme of attack was much too short. The enemy's artillery started shelling LOOS and part of Hill 70 at 8am. At 8.30am our own guns so effectively shelled B Coy that they were unable to get into position, and any attack by this Coy. was out of the question. A Coy was unable to advance owing to the guns not having cut down the German wire in front, which at this spot was particularly strong. Major MacPherson and Captain Robertson were killed immediately, they got out over our parapet in front of C Coy, and then the whole assault fizzled out, it was not likely that guns, which had not registered, would accomplish in half an hour what four days bombardment and forty minutes of gas was considered necessary for on the 25th.*

Elsewhere the leading wave struggled to move forward to assault

Scottish troops look on as artillery shells have little effect on the German trenches.

amongst the confusion. To make matters worse the mist, that had up to now hampered operations, began to lift just when the Scots needed it most. Meanwhile, 200 men of the 178th Regiment holding the redoubt braced themselves for attack.

Despite their difficulties the Scots advanced punctually. The entry in the war diary of the 7th Royal Scots Fusiliers briefly describes the attack:

> *Assault delivered by our first line at 9.00am failed, our guns firing short caused some men on left and centre of line to turn. The line was rallied, advanced again but could not capture redoubt. Casualties heavy.*

The story was repeated all along the front. As soon as the charge was sounded a heavy crossfire swept the summit. With the Germans holding a continuous line from Chalet Wood to Loos Crassier such a small attack was doomed to failure. Again though, the Scottish fighting spirit pushed them on to the redoubt. Brutal hand-to-hand fighting followed and for a time it seemed as though the redoubt would fall. Part of the garrison ran, and even though their numbers were dwindling fast, the Scots followed. Like their predecessors the day before they found themselves on a bare open slope raked with machine-gun, rifle and artillery fire from every direction. Hardly any

Map 25. 45 Brigade's attempt to clear the summit of Hill 70 on the morning of the 26th.

returned.

Meanwhile, the two battalions of 62 Brigade were moving close to the summit, unaware of the disaster that lay ahead. The men were terrified, never before had they been under fire and now they could see and hear the battle up above. Just as they reached the crest the Scots fell back causing some confusion. The fire was so heavy that hardly any men reached the perimeter of the redoubt. Officers tried in vain to encourage their men forward. Lieutenant-Colonel Arthur Hadow, of the 10th Green Howards leapt forward, shouting 'charge', followed by Major Wilfred Dent, Major Ralph Noye and Captains Thomas Charteris and Joseph Lynch. All were cut down instantly. The attack was over, and for a second time the summit of Hill 70 was carpeted with dead and dying men. Seeing the survivors crawling back, the Germans began to reoccupy the redoubt, bombing down the perimeter trench. By 10.30am they were in full possession of the hill, leaving 45 and 62 Brigades clinging to the shallow trenches below the crest. Where possible men crawled or ran back to safety, drawing fire from every direction. The seriously wounded had to be left behind and they faced a long agonising wait until nightfall. Meanwhile, the men behind the crestline had to listen to their comrades cries for help. Private Robert Dunsire, of the 13th Royal Scots, was determined to assist:

Lying in the fire-swept zone between British and Germans,

Private Robert Dunsire VC.

117

a wounded man moved a limb as if in a despairing appeal for assistance, and Private Dunsire, heedless of the flood of bullets, crawled out to him and brought him back to safety. He had just returned when a shout for help drew his attention to a second wounded man, who was also rescued after a death-inviting sally by Private Dunsire. How he managed to escape without a scratch was a mystery, for the earth was madly dancing to the continuous thud of bullets.

Private Dunsire was awarded the Victoria Cross three months later. Unfortunately he did not survive long enough to enjoy his reward. On 30 January 1916 Dunsire's dugout near Hulluch received a direct hit from a trench mortar. He died of his injuries a few hours later at Mazingarbe Dressing Station. His grave can be found in the Communal Cemetery.

German counterattacks on Bois Hugo and Chalet Wood

To the north, 63 Brigade found itself in a precarious position at dawn. Although it was holding a secure perimeter around the western end of Bois Hugo, its left flank was exposed. Meanwhile, the Germans had moved up under cover of darkness to hidden positions, close to its right flank. At the foot of the slope, to their rear, was Brigadier-General Gloster's 64 Brigade. The brigade had only just arrived and as yet Gloster had not managed to contact Brigadier-General Nickalls. Having spent a long night marching across the battlefield, the men were deployed in readiness for new instructions. Major R B Johnson of the 15th DLI described in a report on his experiences how the men were kept busy. His men were:

...formed into a line facing approximately south along a fragmentary and very shallow German trench. A Company on the left, B. C. and D. Companies extended to the right. The frontage allotted to the Battalion did not permit all to be in line. B. Company had one platoon in line, the other three were a short distance in rear, where there was no existing trench the men were at once set to work to dig themselves in, and where necessary the front trench was altered and improved as it was originally sited to face our rear. This had to be done with the small entrenching tool each man carried, and took some considerable time.

At 8.00am, just as the mist lifted, the order to support 63 Brigade's advance through Bois Hugo and Chalet Wood at 11.00am arrived. As they waited the men were ideally placed to observe the 9.00am attack on Hill 70 and, so far, it appeared that everything was going to plan.

Puits 14 bis with Bois Hugo on the horizon. IWM - Q43109

63 Brigade had been preparing to advance through Bois Hugo when orders came to wait for a general attack all along the front. Major Storey reassured the officers of the 8th Lincolnshires that "All is well. The advance will commence at 11.00am". Soon afterwards they observed a large number of Germans retreating to the south. Opening fire, they shot many, but in doing so disclosed their positions. Before long the German artillery retaliated, showering Bois Hugo with shrapnel. Infantry followed, moving forward through the wood. The brigade war diary illustrates how the Germans began to pressurise the Lincolnshire battalion:

At 9.30am the Colonel Commanding the Regiment on the right of PUITS 14 BIS reported verbally to the Brigadier that the situation was distinctly unfavourable, that the Germans were pushing through in large numbers and suggesting that we should ask for support.

While engaging 63 Brigade, the Germans also attacked Chalet Wood, 200 metres to the south. The 6th Cameron Highlanders, led by Lieutenant-Colonel Angus Douglas-Hamilton, had held the wood overnight, but by dawn were exhausted and running low on ammunition. Elements from three German regiments eventually cleared the Scots from the wood, driving them back across the Lens road. Undeterred, Douglas-Hamilton led his men back into the wood time and time again, each time his party diminishing in size. Finally, with only around fifty of the Camerons still capable of standing they followed their leader into the undergrowth for the last time. The regimental history describes the gallant officers last moments:

> *Four times he led the poor remnant of the Battalion and some 100 others who had rallied around him against the ever increasing enemy now holding Hill 70. Then he sank to the ground with the quiet, natural words. 'Colquhon, I'm done.' 'Of course', said Captain Colquhon to himself 'of course he's done.' He has had the whole thirty hours of cold, hunger and anxiety and he was doubling all these times ten yards in front of us up Hill 70! Then perceiving the facts, the two officers still with him bandaged up his wounds, but twenty minutes later with the words 'I must get up, I must get up', he passed away.*

Lieutenant-Colonel Angus Douglas-Hamilton VC.

Douglas-Hamilton's efforts were ultimately in vain, for the Camerons were wiped out almost to a man, leaving the wood and its commanding view over the Loos valley in German hands. Because of his determined leadership in the face of overwhelming odds, the 52 year-old officer was posthumously awarded the Victoria Cross. In January 1916 the 7th Cameron Highlanders recovered his body, but the grave was lost during later fighting. His name is carved at the head of his men on the Dud Corner Memorial.

Meanwhile, 63 Brigade's position, now isolated on both flanks, began to deteriorate rapidly. Efforts to reinforce Chalk Pit Wood with two companies of the 10th York and Lancasters only added to the confusion.

> *The order was apparently misunderstood and the whole Regiment not only went to the Wood but went beyond it, in some cases companies were lying outside the wood in the open, ten yards from the wood, thereby causing unnecessary casualties.*

Anxious to restore order before the general advance began, General Nickalls sent a request for reinforcements from 64 Brigade, in the hope of maintaining his hold on Bois Hugo. He also instructed his battalion commanders to gather at the Chalk Pit at 10.00am to receive their orders. Lieutenant-Colonel Leggett, 12th West Yorkshires, never made it; he was severely wounded by a shell as he approached brigade headquarters. The battalion commanders were verbally instructed to advance eastwards at 11.00am. Meanwhile, the Germans had other ideas:

> *About 10.30am, after a rather heavy bombardment, a weak hostile advance against our left flank began, against which our artillery made excellent practice.*

Although this counter-attack was driven off easily, it was significant.

The company belonged to the 26th Regiment, the first troops of the 8th Division to arrive on the battlefield. They had marched overnight from Douai. Undeterred, the Germans attacked a second time:

> The enemy debouched from both sides of the Bois Hugo simultaneously, attacking both A, B and C companies of the Lincolnshire and the three companies of the left (the West Yorkshires). The trenches of the latter were overwhelmed, and the surviving occupants fell back in a confused mass to the support trench. Similarly, on the right, A, B and C fell back through the wood.

Seeing the retreat, the 10th Yorks and Lancs fell back, leaving the two companies of the Somerset Light Infantry to fight alone. Lieutenant-Colonel Howard reported how:

> We were all in good spirits and blazed away at the Germans who were coming into full view all the time now...Things began to get warm now and we all took rifles and shot carefully along the wood wherever the enemy debouched, at ranges varying between 400 and 800 yards. Ammunition ran low so we stripped the dead of theirs and got enough to keep going...

During the German attack Brigadier-General Nickalls was killed and his staff captain went missing, later reported killed. A number of attempts to rally the man and attack came to nothing. The Lincolnshires fought bravely, led by their senior officers:

> Captain L Davis led two or three bayonet charges without success. Here Lieutenant-Colonel H E Walter was shot down whilst gallantly calling on his men to go forward with him and attack the enemy. "He stood," said 2nd Lieutenant Cragg, "not knowing what fear was in the midst of a hot fire at close range, forty yards off, calling on us to charge. Just as he had led he fell." Greatly beloved by all ranks of the Battalion for his fine soldierly qualities, his loss was sorely felt.

It appears that the lack of experience caused unnecessary casualties, and in the heat of battle officers and NCOs found their training lacking. The Brigade war diary bitterly reports how:

> During the retirement, Regimental officers and NCOs did not give much assistance in trying to rally the men (there were a few exceptions in the case of officers but the NCOs were useless). No attempt was made to carry out the retirement as a Military Operation, NCOs and men simply retired in any direction and anyhow they liked ...

Even so the casualty figures reflect the severity of the fighting.

Seventy-one officers were killed or wounded in the brigade, and in the case of the 8th Lincolnshires every officer was a casualty. In less than an hour 63 Brigade had ceased to exist as an effective fighting unit, losing over 1,300 of its number.

Nickalls' request for reinforcements had taken nearly an hour to reach Brigadier-General Gloster. As far as he could see, the woods on the horizon were still in friendly hands. The Brigade diary explains:

> At 9-44am, however a note written personally by Br. Genl. Nickalls, timed 8.53am, arrived, saying his right, in the southern corner of the small rectangular wood, was pressed by a German counter-attack and asking for a battalion to reinforce him there. We had seen no indication of any such attack, and to the contrary had just seen our own troops debouch, and successfully advance from this same corner. It was therefore presumed that the necessity had passed. Nevertheless the 14 DLI were at once sent forward with orders to move to the said wood and there act as General Nickalls might require.

Lieutenant-Colonel A S Hamilton's battalion, consisting of young miners (as was the majority of the brigade), climbed out of its shallow trench and moved up the slope towards Bois Hugo. Just as it reached the Lens highway;

> ...An extraordinary thing happened. Without any apparent attack, or change in the situation, the 63 Inf Bde troops holding the line northward of the house at the northern end of the wood, the house in which Gen. Nickalls had his H.Q, suddenly rose and retired from their trenches.

The 14th Durham Light Infantry then found themselves under attack by their own troops. In a state of panic 63 Brigade believed that they had been outflanked around the south and west outskirts of Bois Hugo. 64 Brigade diary attempts to explain how the misunderstanding occurred;

> ...They apparently took them for Germans owing to their wearing long greatcoats, and made a change of direction as if to attack the 14th DLI in the flank. Then discovering their mistake, and infecting the 14th DLI with their retirement, they and the 14th began retiring together.

The bid to secure Bois Hugo had failed, and in the confusion the Germans were able to consolidate their positions. With both woods in German hands the Scots holding Hill 70 were in danger of being outflanked. Their exposed trenches near the summit came under accurate machine gun fire and for a time it seemed as if the hill would have to be evacuated.

Attempts to retake Bois Hugo and Chalet Wood

With 11.00am quickly approaching, the situation in the centre of IV Corps front was deteriorating rapidly. Help was at hand for away to the west thousands of troops could be seen advancing over the Grenay Ridge; 24th Division's attack was finally underway. Major Johnson of the 15th Durham Light Infantry watched the impressive sight from the foot of Hill 70:

> We watched through field glasses, as if on manoeuvres, wave upon wave of battalions in extended order move at right angles across our front about a mile away. Starting near the northern end of Loos we followed their progress intently and critically until we lost sight of them behind the wood [Bois Hugo], or folds in the ground. The scene was fascinating and exciting because we could not see what happened. There was no sign of battle; no noise, no bursting shells, no enemy in sight, just like an Aldershot field-day with troops in wonderful alignment for the most part. Very critically we scanned the long lines, and wondered what their objective could be. It was an imposing sight.

Meanwhile, time was running out for Brigadier-General Gloster's brigade. The 14th Durham Light Infantry had rallied at the foot of the slope, having quickly recovered from the shock of being attacked. In order to conform to his orders, Gloster ordered the 14th, with the 15th Durham Light Infantry in support, to advance east immediately. However, for some inexplicable reason, the Durham men moved south-east, advancing by short rushes up the slope leading towards the summit of Hill 70. This misdirection could be attributed to the angle of the deployment of the battalions, or even to the slope of the ground. 64 Brigade diary presents an explanation;

> ...it looked as if the hill had been entirely evacuated, especially as our own guns now again began to shell everything on it indiscriminately; and the fact that our troops remaining on the hill were wearing blue smoke helmets aided the illusion that none but Germans were on the hill.

To inexperienced soldiers, with little idea of where they or the enemy were, the battlefield was a confusing place. As 64 Brigade waited to advance they watched their artillery bombard the hilltop and the distant figures scurrying for cover. With their greatcoats and smoke helmets pulled back on their heads the Scots were mistakenly thought to be Germans. When long range fire directed from Hill 70 began causing casualties among 64 Brigade, their minds were made up. The fire was

64 Brigade advanced at an angle across the slope towards the Scots, Chalet Wood is on the horizon to the left. IWM - Q43110

actually overshooting from the redoubt, aimed at the Scots.

As the two Durham battalions moved up the slope towards the imaginary enemy, they inadvertently exposed their left flank to the real threats hidden in Bois Hugo and Chalet Wood. Major Howard describes how the 15th Durham Light Infantry reacted to the changing situation as it crossed the Loos-Hulluch road:

For the first time I became aware of two more woods on our left flank, from which direction with each advance the firing very greatly increased; we were enfiladed by rifle and machine-guns. This was entirely unexpected, and a little disconcerting. Examining the position through glasses I believed I could locate machine-guns in an upper storey of a house on the edge of the middle wood (Bois Hugo I find it is named), and finding A and B Companies somewhat ahead I formed line half left, to face the woods with the object of assisting those who followed. The din was extraordinary, and I found it impossible by shouting my loudest to make my voice carry as far as the third man from me. Crawling along the line, and passing on the order I directed fire upon the windows of the house. These were our first shots of the war, and were fired at a long range. Whilst trying to get more

*men forward, and stopping
wounded men dribbling back I was
myself wounded.*

Bewildered by the chaos of battle, the
Durham battalions began to waver. The
ludicracy of the Scots predicament on
the hill is summed up in the 13th Royal
Scots war diary:

*About 11.30am the situation
became further complicated by the
21st Division advancing to the
attack. They crossed the LOOS-
HULLUCH Road and established a
firing line from which they
proceeded to pour a heavy fire into
the left of the 45th Bde. and Hill 70
causing heavy casualties. However
by establishing some machine guns
near Puits 14 the enemy came to the
assistance of the 45th Bde. by
enfilading the 21st Divn., causing the latter to retire.*

Enfiladed at short range by machine-guns and rifles, the two Durham
battalions lost heavily. With casualties mounting the lines began to
waver, and as they neared the trenches held by the Scots on top of Hill
70 their limit of endurance was reached. Those able to do so ran down
the hill back to where they had started. As the men retreated down the
slopes they were met by fresh troops moving forward, Brigadier-
General Mitford's 71st Brigade was advancing up the slope past the
Chalk Pit:

*This unique spectacle was presented of the larger portion of
the Regiments of (63rd) Brigade retreating through portions of
the advancing battalions.*

While the Durham battalions carried out their fruitless attack,
Brigadier-General Gloster was holding a crisis meeting with
Lieutenant-Colonels Lynch and Pollock, commanders of the 9th and
10th KOYLIs. The intention was for them to renew the advance with as
many rallied men as possible. However, events overtook the officers.
Urged forward by a desire to attack, the 9th KOYLIs advanced;

*...they poured over the top without word of command, like
colts at a starting gate that break the tape and get down the
course before the starter's flag is down.*

In their eagerness to reach the unseen enemy the KOYLIs surged forward up the slope before orders could be issued. The Brigade war diary explains what happened next:

> *It has not yet been discovered who ordered them forward. It was impossible to stop them, and with a few hurried verbal instructions their CO ran off after them. But practically they went off without orders. The 10th KOYLI were hastily ordered to follow in support, and their CO was ordered not to go beyond the LOOS-HULLUCH road. There was no prospect of two battalions succeeding where many had failed, and it was hoped merely to restore morale by ending up in advance of some kind, and then dig in near the road beyond which further advance seemed impossible.*

Every able-bodied man in the Loos valley joined the advance forward, which again moved towards the summit of Hill 70. For a second time the Scots holding out near the crest found themselves under attack by their own countrymen. Not surprisingly the two KOYLI COs were unable to arrest the movement of so many. Only the two support companies of the 10th KOYLIs received the order to halt in time. The men of the 106th Reserve Regiment watched in amazement from Bois Hugo and Chalet as:

> *Masses of infantry, estimated at about a division, began to advance in about twenty waves on a front between Loos and Chalk Pit Wood, moving in a southerly direction towards Hill 70. Simultaneously those British troops entrenched opposite Hill 70 Redoubt opened a heavy covering fire. The advancing masses were nevertheless taken under fire by the machine-guns and rifles in the Hill 70 redoubt and effectively enfiladed by those of the 153rd Regiment and a company of the 106th Reserve Regiment....The effect of this fire from two sides was very considerable, whole lines being mown down by the machine-guns. The conglomeration of units were crumpled up by flanking enemy machine-gun fire and shrapnel, and retired.*

By 11.00am 64 Brigade was finished as an effective formation. Gloster's command had suffered over a 1000 casualties in its futile attempt to drive the Scots from Hill 70. The majority of the survivors fell back to the trenches of Grenay Ridge, leaving the two reserve companies of the 9th and 10th KOYLIs to hold the line immediately north of Loos. Meanwhile, the Germans watched unmolested from Bois Hugo and Chalet Wood.

Chapter Eleven

24th DIVISION'S ATTACK ON THE GERMAN SECOND LINE

71 & 72 Brigades advance

Brigadier-General Betram Mitford's 72 Brigade had spent an uneasy night in the German trenches east of Lone Tree. It was the men's first experience of battle and they restlessly waited, watching and listening to the battle around them:

> At times there was fair visibility, for the enemy bombardment of Loos had turned the village into a furnace of flame, with Tower Bridge silhouetted in black outline against the ruddy glow, and the sky was lightened by other burning villages, shellfire and Very lights. From time to time would come a wave of mist, when all was hidden.

As dawn broke Brigadier-General Mitford, concerned at the lack of information, sent Major Sir W Kay to Vermelles in search of instructions from divisional headquarters. For nearly five hours the men waited, hidden by the mist while the battle raged all around. Major Kay returned at 9.45am with verbal orders to advance east to attack the German second line. Although written confirmation had been sent it did not arrive until nightfall. It read;

> 1st Division attacks Hulluch 11am, 72 Brigade to attack second line trench between Puits 13 bis (south-east of Hulluch) and the redoubt exclusive, 21st Division will attack on your right against redoubt and continuation of the trench south of it to Bois Hugo. The attack will be preceded by an artillery bombardment. The attack will cross the Lens - La Bassée road at 11am.
>
> From 24th Division, 7.10am.

The dearth of information is astounding. With no details on what the objectives were, or information on the German positions, the brigades were expected to walk forward and through the German lines. With time running out, Mitford had no opportunity to plan the proposed attack. With minutes to spare he summoned his battalion commanders, as related in the Royal West Kent Regimental History:

> At about 10.20am Colonel Vansittart was sent for by the Brigadier and got orders to attack at 11am; he reached the battalion again at 10.53, and only had time to give orders for the whole Battalion to move up into the fire trench, and tell off

companies as firing line and supports. We were told that there were plenty more fellows in reserve to go through us, and that the troops on either flank would attack simultaneously with ourselves.

Despite the last minute rush 72 Brigade advanced punctually. Two battalions led the advance, the 8th Royal West Kent on the left, and the 9th East Surreys on the right. 8th Queens followed in support on the left with the 8th Buffs to the right. The 2nd Welch watched the attack develop from their trenches in front of Hulluch:

We saw a marvellous sight. Line upon line of men in extended order came over the crest of the hill behind us and advanced down to the HULLUCH - LENS ROAD and then up towards the German line of trenches on the crest of the rise.

In awe of the unreal experience the men advanced silently straining, under the weight of their packs. The Kent Battalion went directly east, with their line of advance directed to the south of Hulluch, in the belief

Map 26. 24th Division prepares to advance towards the German Second Line, as 21st Division falls back from Bois Hugo and Chalet Wood.

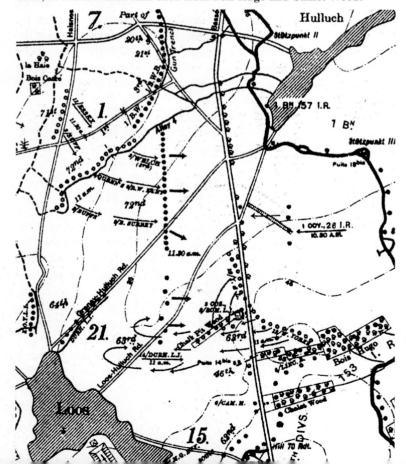

that troops of 1st Division were preparing to assault it. However, less than a hundred men of the 2nd Welch participated; the remainder did not receive the order to attack until it was too late.

The attack was carried out at a marching pace in order to save the men's breath for the final charge and bayonet work, and the advance was so steady and formations so regular that it looked more like a field day at Aldershot than part of a great battle. The enemy brought a very heavy rifle fire, machine-gun and artillery fire to bear on the attacking lines, and shortened his range to keep pace with the advance with wonderful precision; but the casualties up to this point, though severe, were not inordinately heavy.

Meanwhile, the East Surreys were forced to march south-east to extend the brigade frontage in line with divisional orders. As they swung eastwards to cross the Lens Road they witnessed the retirement of 63 Brigade from Bois Hugo. Undeterred the East Surreys continued and their steady advance contributed to the rallying of the broken brigade.

As 72 Brigade deployed it became obvious that the divisional order had an inherent flaw. The designated frontage was in excess of 1500 metres wide, yet each battalion covered only 400 metres. In their attempts to conform to their orders the Royal West Kents and the East Surreys drifted apart leaving a 700 metre gap in the centre of the brigade. General Mitford immediately reacted, sending forward the 8th Buffs, under command of its sixty-four year old Lieutenant-Colonel, Frederick Romer CB CMG. The previous day Romer had addressed his men at Bethune:

I am not going to make a speech to you, but only to ask you to remember that you are the Buffs.

Moving forward at the double the ranks extended out into artillery formation in response to the German shelling, taking their place at the centre of the line. Lieutenant-Colonel Romer, in common with many battalion commanders at Loos, led his men from the front. He was one of the first casualties, hit in the shoulder. Despite the wound he continued forward until shot through the heart and killed.

As the leading lines approached the Lens - La Bassée Road the men were greeted by a cheering sight, as recalled in the 2nd Welch war diary:

All the Germans who had advanced to attack us, on seeing these men advance, they turned round and ran as hard as they could up the hill throwing away all their arms and equipment and finally disappeared through their barbed wire and into their

The area south of Hulluch, the trees mark the line of the La Bassée road. Vendin-le-Vieil colliery dominates the horizon. IWM - Q43105

trench. Many were shot down as they retreated, but many more escaped. Some headed north, taking refuge in the trenches around Hulluch village, others took cover in a sunken road which ran along the northern edge of Bois Hugo.

Events now began to unfold rapidly all along the front. As the Royal West Kents crossed the Lens Road on the left two companies of the 2nd Welch rose from their trench and joined the advance.

A very severe machine-gun fire from either flank swept the road, and very heavy casualties were sustained in crossing it. About four hundred yards east of the road the Battalion passed a forward German trench full of enemy dead. As the advance swept up the long slope towards the main German trenches the machine-gun fire increased in intensity, being very severe from both flanks. Shelling directed from behind Hill 70 and from the south-eastern part of Hulluch was also very heavy, and two field guns were brought up to a position from which they took the attack first from the flank and later from the left rear, firing practically over open sights.

Despite the terrible onslaught the advance continued, officers and sergeants encouraging the men forward. Many were hit (twenty four out of twenty five officers were casualties), trying to keep order among the thinning ranks.

Meanwhile, the half battalion of Welsh, on the extreme left reached the wire on the southern outskirts of Hulluch. The Welch's war diary recalls how victory appeared to be imminent:

...they managed to get through with ease and enter the German trench which was practically unoccupied. The few Germans who were to be seen were unarmed and desirous of

surrendering. The corps on our right also reached the German wire and we all thought that at last we had gained what might be called a real victory, as according to all maps this line was the last line of defence and we had vision of advancing many miles.

The Royal West Kents, however, had not been so fortunate. On their front between Studzpunkt III and IV, the barbed wire was found to be undamaged, with no visible gaps. Beyond, the trenches were full of Germans firing rapidly into the ranks of approaching men. In places the wire was reached, but it was found to be secured by stakes driven deep into the ground:

Many men made gallant attempts to get through the wire, 2nd Lieut. Don being killed when half-way through. The remainder dropped to the ground where they were and returned the heavy fire from the enemy's trench. The situation, however, was hopeless. In front was an impenetrable belt of wire, and the line, such as was left of it, raked with rifle and machine-gun fire from the front and both flanks, and enfiladed by an equally deadly artillery fire.

To make matters worse, the supporting artillery was firing short, showering the two brigades with shrapnel. Only Lieutenant W K Tillie, the West Kents Battalion machine-gun officer, remained unhurt. The rest, along with over 500 men, lay dead or wounded on the slope leading up to the wire. After the battle Lieutenant-Colonel Vansittart sent a report to the War Office in support of his Battalion:

The 8th Royal West Kents actually got from half to three-quarters of a mile east of Hulluch – that although the fire was very heavy and from every direction, officers and men alike showed not the least semblance of any check or stop. They advanced as if on parade and under perfect discipline till they reached the enemy's undamaged barbed wire entanglement, beyond which they were unable to go; and here our losses were heavy.

Meanwhile, the 8th Queens advanced by short rushes, joining the Kent battalion on its right. It too had suffered heavily, losing over four hundred casualties. The men were in a predicament. Ahead was a thick belt of wire, the trench beyond full of Germans. Behind was an open slope swept by fire of every description. Pinned down with grass their only means of cover, they stayed still, awaiting the promised supports.

The 11th Essex, from 71 Brigade, was following in support, having been ordered forward at 11.25am. Again their orders were unclear:

Towards midday the C.O. simply said '11th Essex get out of

131

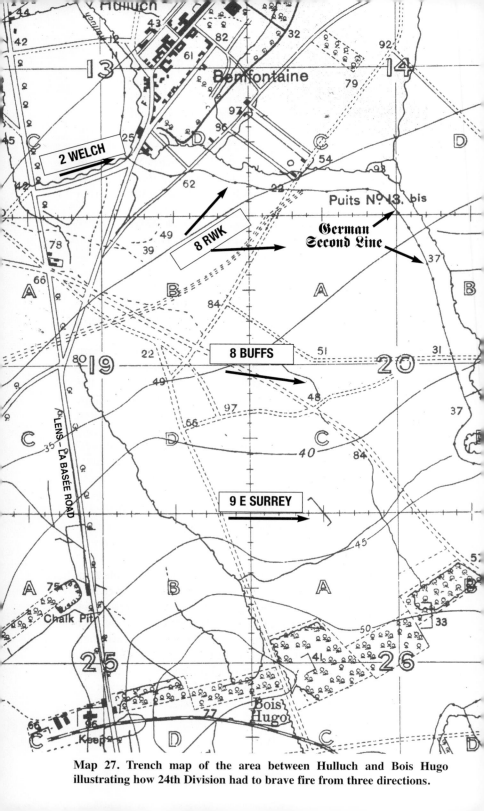

Map 27. Trench map of the area between Hulluch and Bois Hugo illustrating how 24th Division had to brave fire from three directions.

the trench' and the word was passed along, followed by the order,
'Artillery formation to the right'.

By now the Germans were alerted to the threat to their front and, with the leading battalions pinned down, they were able to turn their attentions to the Essex.

As the Essex went down the forward slope to the low ground through which ran the main Lens - La Bassée road, first fire from field guns and then machine-guns opened upon them in enfilade, sited apparently in and around Hulluch village. The commanding officer, Lieutenant-Colonel Radclyffe - leading the Battalion, cane in hand and with a small dog barking at his heels - the second in command, Major Davies and the Adjutant, Captain Heppell, wounded, all went down within a few minutes before the machine-gun fire which rattled like a mowing machine.

After crossing the Lens road the battalion split into two. The left hand companies drifted towards Hulluch in a gallant, but futile, attempt to enter the village. The remaining two companies followed the route of the Kents and Queens. As an Essex officer wrote afterwards:

The bearing of the men was splendid, everyone was as cool as possible. As good as a peace parade, and better. The excitement made it better...We thought we were only moving in support. We never knew where we were. That dreadful lost feeling is one of the worst things to face in war.

In just over an hour, three and a half battalions had been thrown at the defences south of Hulluch, and each one in turn had been destroyed. Over a 1000 men lay scattered, pinned down on the slope south of the village. Twice as many were dead or grievously wounded, with no chance of rescue. Corporal G W Chase echoes the feeling of helplessness and confusion of those still alive:

New experiences: bewildering and terrifying; men destroyed; bursting shells; carnage, shambles; time counted for nothing.

Leaving this sector for the moment, it is time to follow the fortunes of the right half of 72 Brigade in its advance north of Bois Hugo. The 9th East Surreys kept perfect formation as it climbed the gentle incline to the north of Chalk Pit Wood, partially concealed until it crossed the Lens road at the top of the slope. Snipers hidden amongst the trees lining the Lens highway targeted the officers. Captain Herbert Dealtry was killed and Captains Collinson and Charles Barnett died of wounds. Major Howard Welch and Captain Wilfred Birt were also hit, both dying of their wounds in captivity. As soon as C and D companies crossed the road, the rifle and machine-gun fire intensified. The

The southern limit of 24th Division's attack, after crossing the La Bassée road the men came under fire from Bois Hugo on the right. IWM - Q43107

Surreys had expected support on their right flank, with 64 Brigade clearing Bois Hugo. Instead a number of German machine-guns lined the edge, enfilading their flank from close range. In response the men on the right took cover, trying in vain to form a firing line to silence the hidden guns. The remainder pushed on, moving in short rushes:

> *...Right up to the enemy's trenches, but the wire not being cut it was impossible to get through the enemy's lines, although several fruitless attempts were made. The casualties were very heavy at this point chiefly owing to some machine-guns which formed a heavy crossfire on our men.*

The 8th Buffs, with the 9th Suffolks following, also pushed forward towards Stutzpunkt IV in the centre of Brigadier Mitford's front. The Germans were astonished by the weight of the attack, but their morale never wavered. In fact when they saw that their barbed wire was impenetrable their confidence grew as confirmed in the diary of No. 26 Regiment:

> *The battalion staff was on the left flank, south of Stutzpunkt IV, whence we had a wonderful view. The English attacked in whole hosts and with great dash. Our men fired standing up as fast as they could pull the triggers. No Englishmen got through the wire entanglement, and the ground in front was covered with bodies.*

71 and 72 Brigades' Retreat

By 12:30pm the attack had ground to a halt close to the German wire. Faced with an uncut belt of wire and under a murderous crossfire the men of the 24th Division were pinned down. The combined force

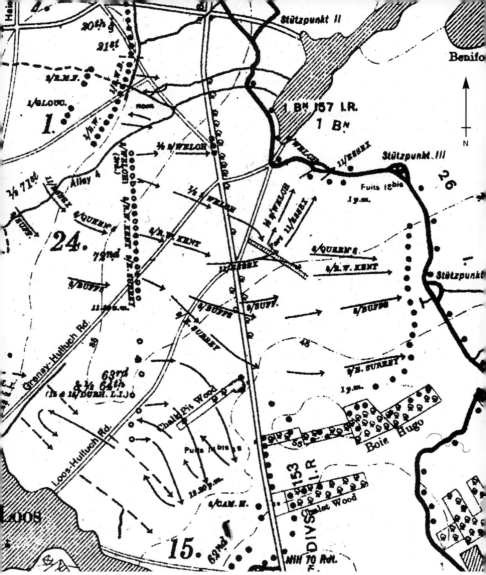

Map 28. 24th Division approaches the German Second Line, meanwhile, 21st Division 'attacks' the Scots on the summit of Hill 70.

of six battalions had suffered over 2,500 casualties, including 100 officers, in just over an hour. With no more reinforcements to deploy, General Rawlinson's attack was over. It would be only a matter of time before the lines began to waver.

The small party of Welch that had penetrated the German line south of Hulluch were forced to retire. Part of the 11th Essex had found refuge in a sunken road south-west of the village. From this haven they attempted to harass the Germans holding the village.

> *The machine gunners were particularly cool and the highest praise is due to both officers and men...They did a lot to keep down the German fire; and were probably chiefly responsible for the Germans not counter-attacking after we were beaten off. During the withdrawal they moved into the gully (sunken road), where they continued to fire, with the exception of the left gun, which moved straight back. No. 3 team took up a position above the bridge in the gully, where it was badly shelled and the gun abandoned, as it was quite useless. The other two were stationed below it and one of them fired three or four hundred rounds with a broken piston rod quite easily...*

Meanwhile a mixed force comprised of the 8th Royal West Kents, 8th Queen's and the rest of the 11th Essex were pinned down in front of the line north of Stutzpunkt IV. Here the fire slackened as the men hid in the long grass. A few gallant soldiers crawled forward to try and cut through the wire. They were confronted with an impossible task. Stout stakes driven deep into the ground were found interlaced with masses of barbed wire. Anybody who was seen was shot down immediately. The gentle slope between Hulluch and Bois Hugo was strewn with the dead and dying, while the wounded attempted to crawl to safety. Captain A K Fison of the 11th Essex recorded his own painful journey back, typical of hundreds of others:

> *I was hit in the right arm by a rifle bullet. The wound was soon bound up by a private of the West Kents who happened to be near. There appeared no good to be done by either going on or staying where I was, so I started trying to crawl back. This soon proved too painful and the only practical method seemed to be to double in short rushes from one shell-hole to another. This process ultimately brought me to the Loos - Hulluch road, after*

A thick belt of barbed wire, impossible to cut though. IWM - Q28970

being shot at more than I cared for, and here I was glad to strike
the beginning of a communication trench, I got slowly along this,
progress being very slow owing to its being full of wounded,
mostly badly hit and waiting for stretcher bearers.

Although estimates vary, it appears that the situation remained deadlocked for over an hour. As time passed it became obvious that there were no more reinforcements. The few remaining officers faced a dilemma. Some were opposed to the idea of pulling back having come so far, after all reinforcements were following. The rest realised that to stay would inevitably lead to death or capture. With so few NCOs to steady the men, the decision was eventually taken from them. What really happened will probably never be known. The Official History places the blame on an anonymous individual shouting retire, an option taken by as many as possible. Inevitably many wounded men would have struggled to make their way back. From their exposed position near the German wire this rearward move could easily have been mistaken for a general retirement.

According to 71 Brigade's report the 8th Queens and 8th Royal West Kents began to retire at about 1.30pm and Brigadier Mitford at once took steps to prevent it turning into a full-scale rout:

Endeavours were made to stop this by sending a company of
12th Sherwood Foresters to the left. Captain G E Hope, Staff
Captain and Captain H.D.M James machine gun officer, both of
the 71st Bde. Staff were sent to the left with the result that the
retirement was stopped at the captured German trenches.

There are conflicting accounts as to whether the retirement was made in good order or not. According to the Official History the men,

began to fall back steadily, without panic and at even pace,
towards the Lens Road.

However, the report in the 2nd Welch war diary is damning. From their trenches west and south of Hulluch they watched the retreat unfold:

But suddenly to our amazement and disgust the whole Corps
on our right turned round and bolted in a wild panic. The men
threw away their rifles and equipment and ran back across the
valley and disappeared over the crest of the hill over which they
had advanced so magnificently. In this rout they all bunched
together and so made a good mark for the German shrapnel and
machine-guns in HULLUCH and consequently lost twice as
many as they did advancing. We were left with two companies
opposite HULLUCH, an impossible situation to remain in as we
had both flanks in the air and had no support, so we retired

slowly but naturally losing heavily. Eventually the remnant of us, some 150 men with seven officers, arrived in the trench we started from. Here we remained in comparative quiet.

The contempt shown by regular soldiers towards 'Kitchener's men' is very apparent.

Meanwhile, the 9th East Surreys had been retiring slowly from Bois Hugo. Seeing the general retreat to their left, they naturally joined it, taking the 9th Suffolks with them. Again, Brigadier Mitford took steps to stop the retreat, and form a line in the German trenches west of the Lens - La Bassée Road. Unfortunately, this time it was too late:

Soon after this much greater retirement of troops was observed on the right. It had proceeded too far to stop it at the captured trenches and Brigadier General M. Shewer and Major

Map 29. IX Corps attack is over, 21st Division and 24th Division retire from the battlefield.

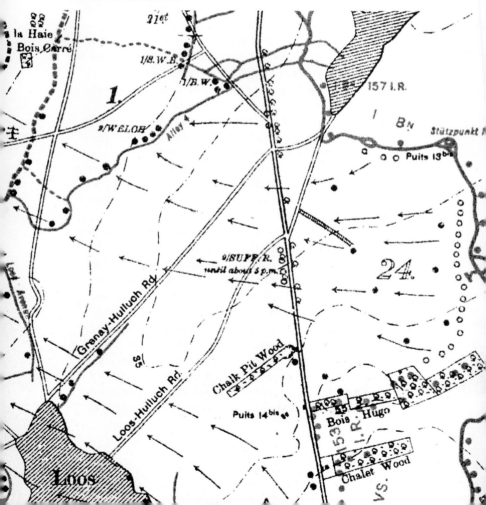

H.C.D. Jowett, Brigade Major 71 Brigade, proceeded to that part of the field and succeeded to a large extent in arresting this movement at the original British trenches in the vicinity of Lone Tree.

By now virtually all of the 21st and 24th Divisions were in retreat, leaving the area between Hulluch and Bois Hugo strewn with dead, dying and wounded men. Brigadier-General Mitford's 72 Brigade had suffered nearly 2000 casualties, and the two battalions of 71 Brigade had lost a further 700. The advance had achieved nothing.

The retirement left several parties of unwounded men, totalling about 500. Many of the 8th Buffs, were stranded close to the German line near Bois Hugo. With little chance of moving either backwards or forwards, they remained hidden in the tall grass or sought shelter in shell holes. Engaging in sniping at the German trenches, these scattered parties prevented the Germans from launching a counter-attack. Second Lieutenant Philip Christison of the 6th Cameron Highlanders, lying wounded in a shell hole, watched as the Germans tried to pursue 72 Brigade:

But one stout fellow, Sergeant A.F. Saunders, refused to retire. He had a Lewis gun he had picked up with a full drum on it. He crawled over to me and said he'd stay and fight. He made to crawl over to the next shell hole and, as he did so, a shell landed and blew part of his left leg off about the knee. I crawled over and got him into a shell hole, putting a tourniquet on his leg and giving my water bottle as his was empty. I crawled back to my hole and a few minutes later...saw a fresh wave of Germans troops advancing...There seemed to be no point in opening fire as there were, perhaps, 150 enemy advancing rather diagonally across our front. To my amazement, I heard, short sharp bursts

The centre of the 'Field of Corpses'. By mid afternoon hundreds of men were falling back in disarray, nearly three thousand lay dead or wounded beyond the La Bassée road. IWM - Q43106

of Lewis gun fire coming from the shell hole to my right; this was Sergeant Saunders, more or less minus a leg. The Germans were taken by surprise and bunched, so I joined in and between us we took a heavy toll and the rest retired out of sight.

Sergeant Arthur Saunders was eventually rescued, and received the Victoria Cross for his gallant conduct. He died in 1947, aged 69. Christison was awarded the MC and remained in the army, attaining the rank of general.

The battlefield now became quiet, a strange phenomenon after the slaughter. Sickened by what they had seen, the Germans ceased firing. All along their front lay injured men, some calling for assistance, others silent in fear of being shot. Here and there German medics began to emerge and pass through the wire. The war diary of the 2nd Welch describes the scene south of Hulluch:

All our wounded had to be left between the lines. About 2pm the Germans sent out a great many stretcher bearers and RAMC men who worked the whole afternoon binding up our wounded and sending all who could walk or crawl back to us. There were plenty of our shells falling about but although they lost some men these Germans never stopped their work. Directly it was dark we sent out parties to bring in our wounded and we found several men who had been bound up by the Germans and who had left them telling them that if they were not removed before a certain hour they would be forced to take them prisoners.

Sergeant Arthur Saunders VC.

Nobody who experienced the advance of the 71 and 72 Brigades would forget what happened. The strip of ground between Hulluch and Bois Hugo became known to the Germans as *"Leichenfeld von Loos"*, translated as *"The Field of Corpses"*.

General Haig's gamble for a great breakthrough had failed. Many have questioned why he sent inexperienced men forward to what, in hindsight, was a certain death. Unfortunately, this is not the place to discuss the whys and wherefores of the attack. The final word goes to Colonel C. Stewart, GSO 1 21st Division. In 1925 he wrote to Major A.F. Becke and gave the following explanation:

It was that these two divisions would be in reserve in a big operation at Loos on the idea that not having been previously engaged in this way, they would go into action for the first time full of esprit and élan, and being ignorant of the effects of fire and the intensity of it, they would go forward and do great things.

Chapter Twelve

27 SEPTEMBER THE GUARDS DIVISION

The 25 September was a difficult day for Cavan's men, for hours on end the Guardsmen tried to march closer to the front ready to attack. Supply wagons, ambulances and troops moving in every direction barred the way and with insufficient personnel to direct traffic, it was after midnight before they reached Nouex-les-Mines and Houchin. The following afternoon orders called for the Division to take over the line north of Loos. Following the disaster that had befallen the rest of IX Corps, General Haig had been forced to instruct the 3rd Cavalry Division to hold the weakened sector. By midnight 1 and 2 Guards Brigades were holding the Grenay Ridge. 3 Guards Brigade was left in reserve on the Lens – Bethune highway, south of Vermelles.

2 Guards Brigade

The main concern at the end of the second day was the occupation and consolidation of Hill 70 by the Germans. Lieutenant-General Haking and Major-General Lord Cavan were asked to prepare to assault the summit on the afternoon of the 27th. The plan proposed involved a two-pronged assault. The first, by 2 Guards Brigade, would approach the hill from the north via Chalk Pit Wood and Puits 14 Bis. A smoke screen, created by 1 Brigade to their left, would screen the advance from accurate fire from Hulluch.

Two hours before the attack began, news of reversals on I Corps front forced General Haig to scale down the Guards' attack. New orders for a limited assault with the Lens highway as its final objective arrived shortly before zero. The 2nd Irish Guards would lead, with the 1st Scots Guards echeloned behind its right, the 1st Coldstream Guards would follow the Irish Guards whilst two companies of the 3rd Grenadier Guards supported the Scots Guards. The brigade would start from its overnight positions, the German trenches to the west of Loos. They had to cross 1,000 metres of open ground before reaching the German lines. Fortunately, the smoke fooled the German artillery into thinking that the attack was directly on Hulluch. At 4.00pm, following a ninety minute bombardment, the 2nd Irish Guards left their trenches and advanced forward. Their objective was the Chalk Pit and the adjacent strip of woodland.

View across the Loos valley to Chalk Pit Wood. IWM - Q43108

The orders for the Battalion, after a conference and a short view of the ground, were that No. 3 Company (Captain Wynter) was to advance from their trenches when the bombardment stopped, to the southern end of Chalk Pit Wood, get through and dig itself in the tough chalk on the farther side. No. 2 Company (Captain Bird), on the left of No. 3, would make for the centre of the wood, dig in too, on the far side, and thus prolong No. 3's line up to and including the Chalk Pit - That is to say, that the two Companies would hold the whole face of the wood. Nos. 1 and 4 companies were to follow and back up Nos. 3 and 2 respectively.

This advance was carried out with very few casualties under cover of the smoke screen, the men 'keeping their direction and formation perfectly.' The war diary describes how the Guardsmen deployed;

one platoon extended in front as a line of skirmishers and the other three platoons of each company, each platoon in column of fours and separated from one another.

Without too much difficulty Lieutenant-Colonel Butler's men formed an effective firing line along the eastern edge of Chalk Pit Wood, securing the brigade's flank.

Meanwhile, the 1st Scots Guards had crossed the valley at the double, again suffering few casualties. Two companies of the 4th Grenadier Guards under Captain Morrison (they had become lost in Loos, debouching from its north side as the Scots were passing) extended their right. A number of the Irish Guards were swept along with the Scots. Amongst them was Lieutenant John Kipling, son of the author Rudyard Kipling. With their eyes focused on the Puits, they came under fire:

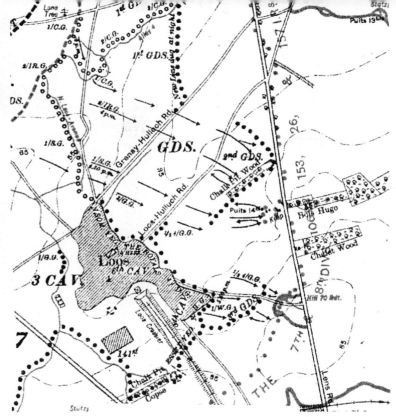

Map 30. The attack of the Guards Division; 2 Brigade advances towards Bois Hugo while 3 Brigade attacks Hill 70.

> *As they then started to move uphill they began to suffer heavily from machine-guns from above the Puits and Bois Hugo in front, and even more from the German trenches on Hill 70*

Isolated on the bare slope the Guardsmen drew the attention of every gun in range. Hundreds were mown down by the crossfire, including Lieutenant Kipling, and many others were pinned down. Only a small party managed to reach the Puits, led by Captain J H Cuthbert of the Scots Guards, along with Second Lieutenant Crabbe and half a dozen Grenadiers. For a time they fought on, reinforced by a platoon of the 3rd Grenadier Guards under Lieutenant Ayres-Ritchie, but without further help, Cuthbert's men fell back.

A general retirement followed. Many sought cover in Chalk Pit Wood causing considerable confusion amongst the Irish Guards;

> *...shortly before 5pm the men in and beyond the PUITS commenced to retire, and fell back into and through CHALK PIT WOOD in some confusion. The C.O. and adjutant went forward through the wood to clear up the situation, and while going*

through the wood Capt. and Adjutant the Honourable T Vessey was wounded and carried away. Almost at the same moment, and before the C.O. had reached the further edge of the wood, the men from the PUITS came streaming back through the wood, followed by a great part of the Irish Guards line which had been digging in on the further side of the wood. Efforts to stop them in the wood or on the rear of the wood proved futile, but the line was reformed along the HULLUCH-LOOS road.
As darkness fell the Irish Guards retraced their steps, they spent the night consolidating Chalk Pit Wood. Their war diary recounts the difficulty time spent there:

> *It rained throughout the night. Heavy and accurate shelling throughout the morning. Many shells pitched actually on to the trenches burying many men and blowing a few to pieces.*

3 Guards Brigade

3 Guards Brigade, under Brigadier-General Frederick Heyworth, waited in reserve near Vermelles until 3.00pm. As soon as it received orders to attack Hill 70 the Guardsmen formed up and marched off along the Vermelles-Loos road. Near Loos Road redoubt, on the reverse slope of the Grenay Ridge, the 4th Grenadier Guards and the 1st Welsh Guards deployed into artillery formation. In columns of platoons in fours they marched forward at the double over the crest, presenting an inviting target to every German in range. The advance impressed everyone who witnessed it, Captain G A Brett of the 1/23rd London watched from Cemetery Trench on the western outskirts of the village:

> *Attention was first drawn to them by a sharp increase in the number of German shells passing overhead; then bodies of troops, at whom these shells were directed, were seen advancing over the crest of the high ground around Maroc into the valley. More and more came over the crest by platoons in artillery formation, and the intensity of the shelling increased. Quite quickly the opposite slope took on the appearance of a gigantic*

Welsh Guards moving out before their disastrous attack on Hill 70. IWM - Q17374

moving chessboard as the platoons approached with intervals between them. The steadiness of the march was impressive, and those who thought that Guardsmen were only ornamental soldiers revised their opinions speedily. So inspiring was the sight that scores of the 23rd men of their own accord clambered out of their trenches and, under machine-gun fire, pulled aside wire entanglements and threw duckboard bridges over the ditches to facilitate the way for the Guards when it was seen that they had to pass through their lines.

The two battalions entered Loos, the Grenadiers from the north-west side, and the Welsh from the west. At once they were faced with difficulties in the maze of ruined streets. Gas shells caused confusion amongst the Grenadiers as the men fumbled to put on their masks. One of the casualties was Lieutenant-Colonel Hamilton, a serious blow. Two companies struggled through the blocked streets, trying to find a way out onto the slopes of Hill 70. Meanwhile the remaining two skirted around the northern edge of the village, becoming involved in 2 Guards Brigade attack on Puits 14 bis. The Welsh Guards, under Lieutenant-Colonel Murray-Threipland, had to thread its way through the centre of the village. Major Howard, of the 15th Durham Light Infantry, had passed through Loos twenty-four hours earlier, his description of the village does, however, give an insight into the difficulties faced by the Guardsmen:

The village was full of wounded British, dead Germans and horses, captured guns and scattered parties of men. Shells were hurtling through the air and houses, some exploding, others falling with a flop in the gardens. The whole place looked as if frenzied gangs of house-breakers had been working over-time. Amongst the flying brickbats, clouds of mortar, and heaps of rubble, squads of men were forming up; men were walking about in a nonchalant manner with no trace of hurry or excitement.

With darkness falling, Murray-Threipland led his battalion up the slope of Hill 70, ordering the small force of 4th Grenadier Guards to extend to his left:

I arranged to attack the position the Grenadiers directing on my left, my Prince of Wales' Company with a frontage of two platoons prolonging to the right of the Grenadiers: my No. 3 Coy supporting Grenadiers: my No. 2 supporting Prince of Wales': No. 4 I kept in hand.

At 5.30pm the attack began, under the false impression that 2 Guards Brigade had captured Puits 14 bis. Brigadier-General Heyworth only heard of its failure after it was too late to stop the Welsh Guards. From his headquarters on the reverse slope of the hill, Murray-Threipland waited for news as the sounds of battle raging came from the summit:

I was then for some time without any information: darkness came on in less than half and hour of my attack, and I received no artillery support, but equally had no artillery fire on me, the enemy confining themselves to the shelling of the town and the ground where the other two battalions of the 3rd Brigade were still crossing in artillery formation. The rifle fire on my front was heavy, but from what I could make out, not much return fire by us, which was satisfactory, as darkness was on and the advance and bayonet was the thing. The information not arriving was disturbing me for two reasons; first - that I had no information of the progress of the attack, and secondly, - as I felt sure Captains would have sent information if possible, it tended to show that some or all of them were casualties.

In fact the Guardsmen had advanced up the slope suffering few casualties. However, as soon as they emerged onto the flat summit the Germans had fired star shells illuminating the scene. Machine-gun fire from the front and from near Puits 14 bis to the left cut the advancing Guardsmen to pieces, bringing them to a halt close to the German line. Major Ponsonby was mortally wounded at the head of the Grenadier Guards, and Captain Osmond Williams lay seriously

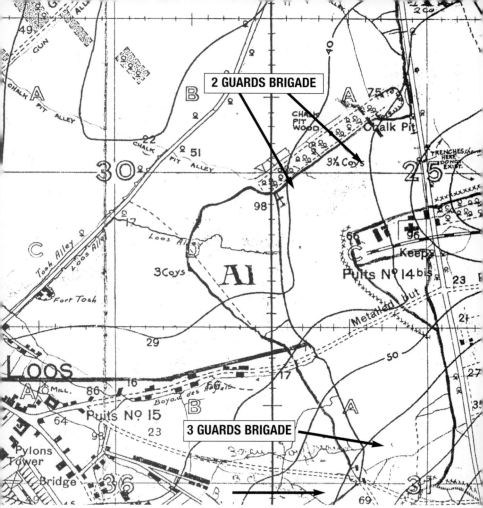

Map 31. Trench map covering the area attacked by the Guards Division.

wounded near the German trenches, surrounded by his Prince of Wales' Company, many of them wounded or dead. The Welsh Guards attack was finished, and although they had advanced to their objective, it was impossible to dig a trench on the bullet-swept summit. Lieutenant-Colonel Cator, of the 2nd Scots Guards, arrived around 11pm with only half his men, the rest were still in Loos, lost in the ruins. Lieutenant-Colonel Murray-Thriepland and Lieutenant-Colonel Cator then visited the summit;

> And it was obvious that no organised digging in could take place on our front line, as fire was too heavy.

The two officers decided to employ the Scots Guards in digging a support trench just below the crest, to which the Welsh could retire

147

before dawn. As Threipland reported, it was an extremely tiring night spent collecting the wounded and recalling the men:

It was very difficult to get our men back, unless I got personally to them, even then they all wanted to go forward and not back. However, we got as many away as possible..... messages had come back from Osmond Williams' line to say they were out of ammunition and, on no less than two occasions, Private Grant of our MG detachment had crawled out with it. Again ammunition was called for, and as it was getting near dawn and not much darker than when Bagot Chester went out, I organised another party to try and get Williams back...I again sent messages for all who could to return, and several slightly wounded and whole ones came back.

Several attempts to rescue officers were made; two men carried Captain Phillips in while his sergeant fought off the Germans with his officer's pistol. Major Miles Ponsonby, acting commander of the Grenadier Guards, was mortally wounded near the German lines, while many of his men never returned, having been cut off. Captain Thorne, the Grenadiers adjutant, was wounded in the head attending to Ponsonby but, seeing that he could do no more for his commander, made his way back:

On the way he came upon two drummers who had been acting as orderlies; one had been killed and the other wounded through

the leg. Knowing that if he left the boy where he was, he would probably be killed, he determined to carry him back. He put him on his shoulders and started off, but must have made some noise, for the Germans at once put a flare up and fired at him with machine-guns. He fell forward at once with the drummer – both killed.

Captain Williams was brought back to safety overnight, but died three days later at Lapugnoy Dressing Casualty Clearing Station. His grave can be found in the Military Cemetery. Ponsonby's body was never recovered and his name appears on the Loos Memorial, as does Captain Thorne's.

Captain Williams DSO, Welsh Guards.

Lieutenant-Colonel Cator's Scots Guards dug in throughout the following day creating a new line along the edge of the summit while engineers wired the position:

Wounded men were continuously crawling back to this little oasis in the desert of shell-holes. Painfully and slowly, inch by inch, these men would arrive, often sniped at by the enemy. It was such an exposed spot that, beyond helping them into the shallow trench, the men in this party could do little.

28 September

A final attempt to take the Puits complex was made on 28 September, with two companies of the 1st Coldstream Guards. This time the attack would start from the cover of Chalk Pit Wood, in the hope that a rapid advance could take the mine buildings by surprise. Not surprisingly, so few stood little chance where so many had failed before, as the war diary reports:

They were met, almost before they got out of their trenches, by a terrific machine-gun fire which enfiladed them from three sides (chiefly from BOIS VICTOR HUGO). They were absolutely mown down. Two officers, Lieutenant Riley and Second Lieutenant Style, with eight men reached the objective, which they found not held by the enemy but only enfiladed by yet another machine gun. Lieutenant Riley (wounded) and two men got back. The men behind behaved simply splendidly, as not only were they subjected to this enormous enfilade fire but also to a most terrific bombardment by 8" shells and shrapnel and every kind of heavy gun fire which was most accurate. Meanwhile No. 3 and No. 4 companies doubled forward to Chalk Pit Wood under fire.

This attack brought the offensive between Hulluch and Loos to an end for the time being. Immediate reserves had been exhausted and with the Germans on the offensive to the north on I Corps front, General Haig needed to deploy his reinforcements elsewhere.

That night the Grenadier Guards machine-gun section witnessed a barbaric act;

.... Lieutenant Williams saw a party of Germans crawl out and advance toward some of our wounded who were unable to move. They appeared to be quite unaware of the handful of men in this trench. Feeling sure they intended to take the wounded prisoners, when their injuries would, no doubt, be dressed, he gave orders that no one was to fire. The Germans crept on slowly, but on reaching the wounded, to Lieutenant Williams' horror, they proceeded to bayonet them. It was hardly necessary for Lieutenant Williams to give the order to fire, as the men with the machine-guns had seen this dastardly act, and the two machine-guns soon wiped out the whole party of Germans.

So the first battle of the Guards Division was over and it was hardly the overwhelming success expected by Rawlinson and Haig. There was, however, little time to rest. A few days later the Earl of Cavan's men were back in the trenches, two miles to the north near Hohenzollern Redoubt.

Chapter Thirteen

TOUR OF IV CORPS AREA

Car Tour

The car tour is designed to give visitors a quick introduction to the area surrounding Loos. It is approximately six miles long, completing a circuit of the battlefield. Many of the roads in the area carrying a great deal of commercial traffic and can be fast and busy, particularly during peak periods. Drivers are advised to concentrate on the road, however tempted they are to take in the scenery. There are occasions when it is possible to park a car safely, but on the main roads it is an offence, as well as extremely dangerous, to obstruct the carriageway.

The sketch map shows the main landmarks and points of interest. This does have advantages as well as drawbacks and it may be wise to study the route on a road map first. Although industry has overrun parts of the battlefield, particularly east of Hill 70, the majority has changed little. Loos itself has

Map 32. Area surrounding Dud Corner.

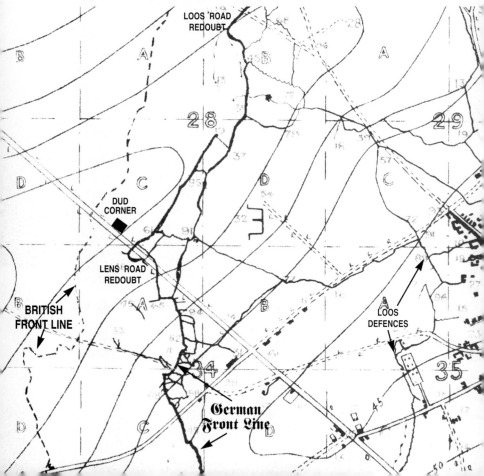

expanded, but the street layout is essentially the same. There are a number of landmarks that become familiar after a while, in particular the twin peaks of the slagheaps that crown the Double Crassier on the southern edge of IV Corps area.

Starting Point: Loos Memorial to the Missing at Dud Corner.

The main route from Bethune to Lens cuts across the centre of the battlefield; the Loos Memorial to the Missing stands alongside as it crosses the top of the Grenay Ridge. To find out about the memorial and the cemetery that it surrounds, consult the Cemeteries section. Standing as it does close to the site of Dud Corner, or Jew's Nose Redoubt, it is an excellent place to start your visit of IV Corps battlefield.

When the memorial was constructed, steps were incorporated into the pavilion to the left of the entrance. The roof of the pavilion is an observation platform, from where it is possible to view the area. The spires of Bethune can be seen in the far distance to the west. The flat top of Fosse 5 slag heap near Maroc, home for many of the British observers, stands to the south west of the road. To the south is where the 47th (London) Division advanced. The Londoners advanced eastwards, obliquely to the road, with their right flank against the twin slag heaps of the Double Crassier. These heaps have been enlarged since 1915. To the east lies Loos village, almost hidden in a small valley. Hill 70, where the 15th (Scottish) Division ended its advance, rises above the houses. Observers on the ridge were able to see the Scots moving up the slopes towards the summit of the hill. Hulluch village,

The German perspective east towards Bethune.

The view south across 47th Division's battlefield.

HULLUCH · **BOIS HUGO** · **CHALET WOOD**

Looking north east from the roof of Dud Corner Pavilion. Hulluch, Bois Hugo and Chalet Wood line the horizon

where 1st Division were halted, lies in a direct line behind the Cross of Sacrifice. Before the battle the German front line ran north and south from Dud Corner, taking advantage of (for the most part) the forward slopes of the Grenay ridge.

If you are unable to climb the steps it is still possible to view 47th Division's sector and across to Loos village from the entrance. By walking to the north eastern end of the cemetery you are able to view 15th Division's sector by looking over the wall beyond the Cross of Sacrifice.

On the morning of 25 September 44 Brigade advanced over the ridge and into Loos. One observer watched anxiously as the Scots swarmed up the slope:

It was magnificent. I could not have imagined that troops with a bare twelve months training behind them could have accomplished it. As the men reached our wire they made their way through it with perfect coolness and deliberation in spite of the enemy's increasingly heavy rifle fire. Once in No Man's Land they took up their dressing and walked - yes coolly walked - across to the enemy trenches. There was no running or shouting; here and there a man finding himself out of line would double for a pace or two, look to his right and left, then take up his dressing and continue the advance at a steady walk. The effect of these seemingly unconcerned Highlanders advancing upon them must have had a considerable effect on the Germans.

The 9th Black Watch, moving parallel to the road, stormed the Redoubt whilst the 8th Seaforths advanced across the ground north of the cemetery. The line immediately south of the memorial was not attacked at zero hour because of the danger of being enfiladed from the redoubt. 44 Brigade's support battalion, the 10th Gordon Highlanders, moved forward an hour later when the redoubt had been cleared. Lieutenant-Colonel Thullier, Chief Engineer of 1st Division,

Looking north along 15th Division's front line from the rear of the cemetery.

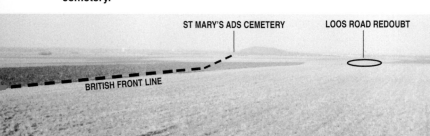

ST MARY'S ADS CEMETERY · **LOOS ROAD REDOUBT**

BRITISH FRONT LINE

visited the area a short time afterwards:

> In front of the remains of the work known as Lens Road redoubt the dead Highlanders in Black Watch tartan lay very thick. In one place about 40 yards square, on the very crest of the ridge and just in from of the enemy wire, they lay so close that it was difficult to step between them. Nevertheless the survivors had swept on and through the German wire.

In June 1917 Thullier joined 15th Division as its GOC and went on to lead it through the Third Battle of Ypres.

Having taken the opportunity to get your bearings, return to your car and head south east, towards Lens. After clearing the Lens Road Redoubt, the 9th Black Watch streamed down the slope to the left of the road, heading for the centre of the village. Take the first right at Valley Crossroads **(A)** signposted for Maroc, (by the petrol station). The London Irish advanced from the crest to the right and after passin gthe Crossroads, headed for Loos Cemetery. No Man's Land ran across the top of the slope to the right. It was one of the few instances when British troops held the high ground.

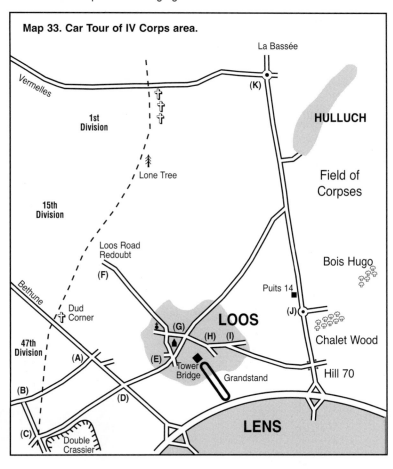

Map 33. Car Tour of IV Corps area.

On the morning of the 25th the 1/7th London chased the Germans down the incline to the left of the road amidst clouds of swirling gas. Half a mile from the crossroads, take the minor road to the left **(B)** heading towards the huge slagheap. The assembly trenches 1/7th and 1/6th London were to the right of the road. Many artillery observers used the slagheap, Fosse 5, behind the Londoners' trenches. At the bottom of the slope, close to the base of the slagheap there is a crossroads **(C)**. 142 Brigade, which carried out the Chinese Attack on the morning of the attack, held the ground directly in front. Turning left follow the base of the slagheap. It has grown considerably in modern times, beyond the confines of the original two strips of ash. Heading east, the road crosses the valley that the 1/7th London crossed on the morning of the 25th. The battalion quickly established a protective flank across the fields to the right of the road. It is important to know that the ground occupied by the 1/6th London has disappeared beneath the slagheap.

Continue to the Lens – Bethune road **(D)** and go straight across, taking particular note of the fast moving traffic, into the centre of Loos. Although the streets are now peaceful, they were once blockaded with barricades. During the early stages of the battle, the men of 1/20th London fought hard to clear the village of Germans. House clearing went onto into the night and it took several days to flush the stragglers out of their hiding places.

The impressive Mairie stands at the centre of village with a car park in front. There is a small store, a bakery and a number of cafes around the square. If you wish to shop for food or drink, make your purchases early. The shops close at noon for an hour and a half and on some days the village is shut all afternoon.

Taking a left turn at the war memorial **(E)**, which names many of the civilians killed in the battle. Keeping the Mairie to your right, continue along the street, the new village church stands to the left on a side road. The 10th Gordon Highlanders entered the village via the houses and gardens to the left, breaking down barriers blocking the streets. Keep straight on to, following the street out of the village. As you pass the last house, the road rises sharply up the reverse slope of the Grenay Ridge. Passing a large farm to your right, keep on to the top of the slope to where the track forks three ways **(F)**. From here it is possible to view the centre of IV Corps battlefield. On a clear day it is possible to see both Dud Corner to the left (south), and St Marys ADS Cemetery to the right (north). Loos Road Redoubt, where Piper Laidlaw piped the 7th KOSBs into action, was a couple of hundred metres along the left hand fork. Turning round, taking care not to stray off the tarmac and get bogged down. The view across the Loos valley is breathtaking on a clear day. Scanning the horizon, from left

Panorama of the Scots advance from the Grenay Ridge. The water tower stands close to the summit of Hill 70.

LOOS VALLEY HILL 70 LOOS CHURCH

to right, it is possible to identify Hulluch, the Field of Corpses, Puits 14 bis (now abandoned mine buildings), Bois Hugo and Chalet Wood. The water tower on the horizon to the south east stands above Hill 70. The Scots managed to advance from this ridge, across the valley, clearing Loos on the way, and over the summit of Hill 70, a distance of over two miles.

Having studied the view, return down the slope returning to the centre of the village. Turn left at the war memorial, keeping the Mairie to your left. Leave the square via Rue Louis Pasteur, with the Bar St Hubert on the left. At the first crossroads **(G)**, 150m from the Mairie, turn right into Rue Kleber, (signposted for Les Tulipiers and the Collége). The 10th Gordon Highlanders had bypassed the square and became intermingled with the 9th Black Watch at this point. Tower Bridge stood behind the buildings to the right and there is now a brick built college on the site. After 150m take the left fork into Rue G Decrombeque **(H)**; a few yards from the junction there is a memorial dedicated to the soldiers that took part in the battle. It is the only memorial in IV Corps area apart from the CWGC memorial at Dud Corner. The memorial stands at the edge of the village as it was in 1915, and beyond this point there were only scattered buildings. Heading away from the centre of the village, take the next right fork **(I)**, Rue Denfort Rochereau, after 100m. A sign post for the École O Leroy points the way.

Memorial to the liberators of Loos.

Heading up the slope through the modern estate, remember that 46 and 44 Brigades climbed up these slopes on their way to the summit of Hill 70. By now the battalions were very inter mixed, and with few surviving officers the two brigades resembled a mob. Two days later 3 Guards Brigade took the same route up the hill. Before long the houses begin to thin out and it is possible to see the open slopes, derelict mine buildings on the horizon to the left stand on the site of Puits 14 bis. Near the top of the slope a line of trees hides the summit from view. The Scots formed a perimeter facing Hill 70 and on the morning of the 26th Private Robert Dunsire VC rescued wounded men under heavy fire from the fields to the left. Passing between the trees, the gradient levels out. The centre of the redoubt occupied the crossroads where there is now a set of traffic lights. Having taken the redoubt in the initial advance, some of the Scots headed south towards Cité St Laurent, now engulfed in the suburbs of Lens. Others headed east towards Cité St Auguste, now hidden beyond industrial buildings. When the Germans counterattacked, the remnants of the two brigades retired beyond the redoubt, Lieutenant Frederick Johnson VC was instrumental in rallying many stragglers. Two further attempts to capture the redoubt, the first on the morning of the 26th and another the following evening by the Guards, failed to take the summit.

Turn left at the traffic lights, following the sign for La Bassée. It is now possible to see what a commanding position the hill affords. Before houses and trees obscured the view across Loos, observers could see across the valley to the Grenay Ridge. The La Bassée road is extremely busy and the lorries travel

The German perspective of the upper slopes of Hill 70, viewed from Chalet Wood.

at speed, so take extra care. Heading down the hill, the slope of Hill 70 to the left of the road becomes apparent. On the morning of the 26th 64 Brigade advanced up the slope to the left towards the summit, having mistaken the Scots for Germans. The large brick building on the right, a crematorium stands in front of Chalet Wood. Lieutenant-Colonel Angus Douglas-Hamilton VC led his battalion repeatedly into the wood. It is possible to appreciate the view that the Germans had as 64 Brigade advanced up the slope.

At the new roundabout continue straight on (**J**). The abandoned mine, Puits 14 bis is to the left, while Bois Hugo is to the right. The western extremity of the wood has been cleared to make way for a light aerodrome. 63 Brigade held the wood on the morning of the 26th, only to be overwhelmed by fierce German attacks. Beyond the wood the landscape opens up to the right, the Field of Corpses. At 11.00am on 26 September, 72 and 71 Brigades began its attack, crossing the road at right angles as it headed towards the German positions. The Second Line ran across the fields to the right, parallel to the road, 1000m away. With Hulluch in front to the right of the road at the foot of the slope, it is easy to see how vulnerable the two brigades were.

Continuing towards La Bassée, 1 Brigade reached the road facing Hulluch at an early stage in the attack. Only a handful of scouts entered the deserted village and by the time assistance arrived, German reinforcements had driven them out. At the mini-roundabout (**K**), turn left for Vermelles. Beyond the housing estate to the left, the fields once more take over. 1 Brigade advanced parallel to the road heading for Hulluch, having suffered grievous casualties storming the German front line. After 3/4 mile, there are three cemeteries in a line to the left of the road. The largest, St Marys ADS Cemetery, stands alongside the road in what was No Man's Land. The two front lines ran directly south, approximately 400 metres apart. The leading battalions of 1 Brigade suffered heavy casualties, from gas as well as from the German guns, before they crossed the wire. Lone Tree, where 2 Brigade and Green's Force were pinned down for nine hours, stood in the fields south of the three cemeteries

Panorama across the Field of Corpses from the La Bassée road.

1000m from the road. Four Victoria Crosses were awarded following the battle at Lone Tree.

Continue past the cemetery affording a brief glance north of the road from where I Corps launched its attack. Vermelles is two miles from the cemeteries. From the centre of the village, head south following signs for Philosophe. The main Bethune - Lens road, the N43, is ¾ mile away. Turning left, sign posted Lens, head back towards your start point 1½ miles away. The Loos Memorial to the Missing stands at the top of the hill, to the left of the road.

Having completed a circuit of the battlefield, you may wish to revisit the viewing platform to reacquaint yourself with the area before deciding which walks to follow.

IV CORPS WALKING TOURS

Walking Tour 1 - 47th (London) Division

Continue south east along the main road towards Lens. Take the first right after half a mile, at 'Valley Crossroads' (1) (there is a petrol station on the right, just beyond the turning). After a short distance pull in on the left by a wayside shrine (2). Leave the car and cross the road, following the tarmac track up the hill. The German front line facing the 19th (London Irish) crossed the road close to the shrine. Where the tarmac track branches left turn round (3) to view the objectives allocated to the 47th (London) Division. On the morning of 25th

Map 34. Walking Tour 1 - 47th (London) Division area.

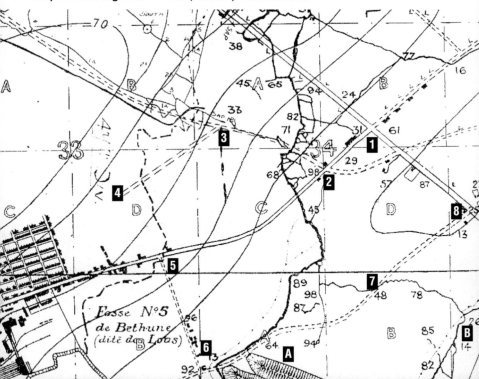

September, the London Irish trench ran across the top of the slope, heading north to south. It was the only sector on IV Corps front where the British held the high ground. To the left the domes in Dud Corner Cemetery can be seen, No Man's Land ran across the field slightly to the left of them.

The London Irish held the line to the right and at zero hour, with the gas rolling down the slope, a football was kicked into No Man's Land. In the distance it is possible to see Loos Church and the town hall. It is important to know that the London Irish advanced at an angle to the Lens road, heading for the southern outskirts of the village. They charged down the slopes heading for the cemetery, which, providing the crops do not hide it from view, is just visible against the edge of the houses.

The twin slagheaps dominate the horizon and they have grown beyond all recognition to those faced by the 1/7th London on the morning of the attack. In 1915, Double Crassier (**A**) was only a fraction of the size, consisting of two long trails of waste from the mine. The lower section of the mountain of ash, now covered in bushes and trees, gives some idea of its wartime height. Directly in front is an open field sandwiched between the village and the slagheap (B). The 1/6th London successfully advanced into the valley, from right to left, establishing themselves in a German support trench that ran across the valley. During the afternoon German artillery, from their positions on the horizon, shelled the valley. There was, however, no attempt to drive the 1/6th London from their positions. The slopes behind and to the right are where 141 and 140 Brigades assembled in preparation for the attack.

Take the left hand tarmac track heading across the top of the slope towards the houses. The front line ran from Dud Corner, obliquely across the slope to the eastern tip of the slagheap. As the track climbs the slope, the flat top of Fosse 7 appears to the right over the horizon. Again it has grown, but in 1915 the flat top provided excellent views across the valley for artillery observers. At the top of the slope, by the houses (**4**), look back to view the southern flank of the battlefield. The direction of the attack was centred on the white water tower, on the far horizon. The London Irish advanced from the high ground on the left into the southern outskirts of Loos, the 1/20th London continuing up the slope beyond to Chalk Pit Copse, close to where the motorway can be seen below the horizon. In the centre, the 1/6th London formed a line across the Lens highway, with the 1/7th London to their right. (The ground held by the 1/7th lies beneath the slagheap.) With the Double Crassier in British hands, IV Corps flank was secured.

The valley south of Loos, the Londoners chased the Germans across the valley.

LOOS VALLEY   HILL 70   CHALK PIT

The southern flank of IV Corps attack, Double Crassier has grown beyond all recognition.

Walk back to your vehicle the way you came, taking time to appreciate the achievements of the London Territorials. Return to the shrine and continue east towards Grenay, taking the first left after a half a mile **(5)**. The road drops sharply down to the tip of the slagheap. Turn left at the crossroads **(6)**, the southern end of the attack, following the base of the huge slopes of slag. After a mile the valley opens up. If time permits park your vehicle and take a few minutes to survey this part of the battlefield from the German point of view **(7)**. Their front line was near the top of the slope to the left of the road, the support line held by the 1/6th London ran across the field to the right. Shortly after zero hundreds of men, their faces hidden by smoke helmets, came down this slope through the clouds of smoke. On the far slope of the valley, holding Chalk Pit Copse to the south east of Loos, was No. 4 Company of the 16th Regiment. From their trenches the men had a perfect view across the valley - that is until the gas release started:

> Smoke and gas clouds rolled up to us across the valley, and were so thick that one could scarcely see for five yards ahead. Suddenly, about 7am, some men appeared on the ridge across the valley, along which lay our front position, followed by dense skirmishing lines. They came down the hill towards Loos, and we thought they were our own infantry retiring, as they appeared to be waving at us with a yellow flag on a long pole. Some of our own troops did pass through us, quite yellow all over with the gas fumes.

Continue in your car crossing the busy Lens - Bethune highway into Loos **(8)**. Many of the London Irish entered the village via this street, on their way to capture Tower Bridge. The village square with its impressive Mairie and car park is the next stop.

The German view of 47th Division's front from the valley. The British front line ran along the horizon.

Walking Tour 2 - Loos Cemetery and Loos Road Redoubt

There are a number of shops and bars situated around the square (1). Be warned; the village closes between 12.30 and 2.00pm, and on certain afternoons. If you intend to have a picnic at some stage buy your provisions early. Before considering the fighting that went on in the village it is time to visit the eastern slopes of the Grenay Ridge.

Look for the CWGC sign for St Patrick's Cemetery to the right of the village war memorial. Follow it, keeping to the main road at the staggered crossroads. The sign for Ecole E Moreau points the way. After a few minutes the neatly cut hedge of the CWGC cemetery comes into view on the right (2). After a visit to the cemetery note the school across the road, named in memory of Emiliene Moreau, the young teacher who bravely assisted the Scots in their battle for the village. Continue to walk along the main street away from the village until the civilian cemetery appears to the left. The oldest section, where the Germans concealed a machine gun in a tomb, is directly in front of the gate. There are signs of shrapnel damage on many graves. To the right is the open reverse slope of the Grenay ridge.

To view the area, walk to the far end of the cemetery wall (3). Immediately in front, looking along the road, is from where the London Irish approached. The petrol station in front (A), stands on the Lens – Bethune road, at Valley

Map 35. Walking Tour 2 - Loos cemetery and Loos Road Redoubt.

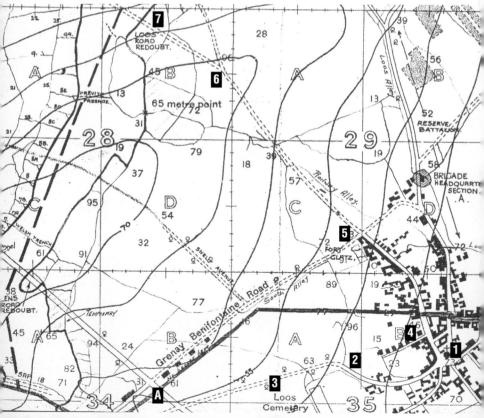

German view from Loos Cemetery, the London Irish's advance started on the horizon.

Crossroads. The London Irish started on the ridge beyond. Meanwhile, the 9th Black Watch came swarming down the open slope to the right of the road.

Heading back to the square, following the route that the Scots took, try to imagine the mayhem on that September morning. Barricades blocking the street were thrown aside, shots were fired from doorways and bombs were tossed through windows as the Highlanders fought their way through the ruins. Back at the square it is possible to see how the 9th Black Watch and the London Irish merged in the square.

Take the road to the left of the Mairie, passing the new church (the original stood in the square on the site of the war memorial) on your left **(4)**. Many 8th Seaforth Highlanders entered the village along the side road, passing to the rear of the Mairie. Others fought their way through the houses and gardens that line the street. Bitter fighting took place around this area and the 8th Seaforth's war diary graphically describes the battle for the ruins:

Loos church, rebuilt at this new location after the war. Many of the 8th Seaforths entered the village along this road.

> The men remaining in the town put up a stubborn resistance, and every house became a kind of little fort, and every cellar a refuge for the enemy. Desperate hand-to-hand fighting naturally went on; units broke up into detachments carrying on individual and isolated encounters; and in the general mêlée men of the different battalions of the Brigade inevitably became mixed.

At the crossroads, where there is a CWGC sign for Dud Corner Cemetery, turn left **(5)**. After a few yards a fine panorama of the Grenay Ridge appears. Fort Glatz stood in the small field to the left of the lane. Its machine gun crew was

The rear slope of the Grenay Ridge as seen from Fort Glatz, the slope was swarming with Scots on the morning of the attack.

well placed to rake the Seaforths as they charged down the open hillside.

Return to the crossroads and turn left heading away from the village, up the slope past a large farmyard. At the top of the slope the track forks into three **(6)**. Take the left hand fork and within a few metres the top of the ridge is reached, provided an excellent view across this part of the battlefield. To the left are the twin domes of Dud Corner memorial, the Scots front line ran from left to right. Away to the right, to the north, three white Crosses of Sacrifice can be seen on a clear day. They stand in No Man's Land in 1st Division's sector. It is quite easy to make out where IV Corps front line ran from here.

Continue west, and after 300 metres the ground begins to drop; this was the site of the Loos Road redoubt **(7)**. The significance of this position is easy to understand, for it commands a perfect view across the British front. The 7th KOSBs advanced up the slope to capture the redoubt, urged on by the skirl of Piper Laidlaw's bagpipes. The low ground to the right of the track is where the 12th Highland Light Infantry crossed No Man's Land, losing heavily in the process. On 30 September 1915 John Buchan, the *Times* newspaper's war correspondent, visited the redoubt:

Beyond the old British front trench you pass through the debris of our wire defences and cross the hundred yards of No Man's Land, over which, for so many months, our men looked at the enemy. Then you reach the German entanglements, wonderfully cut to pieces by our shell-fire. There our own dead are lying very thick. Presently you are in the German front trenches. Here, in some parts, there are masses of German dead, and some of our own. This is the famous Loos Road redoubt, a work about five hundred yards in diameter...t is an amazing network, ramified beyond belief, but now a monument to the power of our artillery. It is all ploughed up and mangled like a sand castle which a child has demolished in a fit of temper. Fragments of shell, old machine-gun belts, rifle cartridges, biscuit tins, dirty pads of cotton wool are everywhere, and a horrible number of unburied bodies.

Returning to the crest it is possible to view the accomplishments of the 15th (Scottish) Division. 46 Brigade entered the valley, advancing north of the village, and onto the La Bassée – Lens highway near the horizon. Hill 70 is slightly to the left of the white water tower, with Chalet Wood to its left. 44 Brigade swept through the village from the right. The twin towers of Tower Bridge stood immediately behind the cream coloured tower of the Mairie, with Loos Crassier beyond stretching up the slope. From this position it is possible to appreciate how much the Scots achieved. As you return to the square picture the slopes filled with soldiers advancing through the morning mist.

Before leaving the village you may wish to see Loos British Cemetery, which is sign posted from the square **(8)**. If so, return to the Mairie after your visit to continue your tour.

The German view over the Scottish trenches from Loos Road Redoubt. Piper Danny Laidlaw piped the 7th KOSB's up the road.

15TH DIVISIONS FRONT LINE

Walking Tour 3 - Loos Valley and the lower slopes of Hill 70

Leave the square via Rue Louis Pasteur, passing to the right of Bar St Hubert. The 8th Seaforths crossed the road heading east, having bypassed the square. Continue out of the village and the Loos valley, which 46 Brigade crossed, can be seen between the houses to the left. A few hundred metres beyond the village, a house stands on its own to the left of the road. There is a memorial, (painted yellow) next to the house **(1)**. Park your vehicle in front of the memorial. The monument remembers six elderly citizens and one wounded French soldier executed by the Germans in October 1914.

Walking back towards the village, cross the road and take the tarmac track that heads up the slope. On the morning of 25 September the 10th Scottish

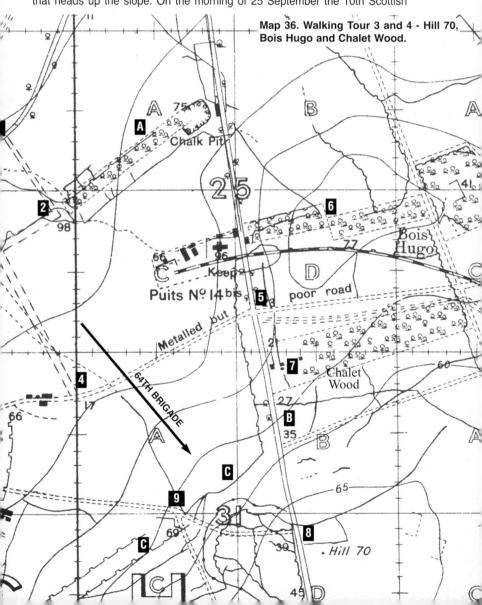

Map 36. Walking Tour 3 and 4 - Hill 70, Bois Hugo and Chalet Wood.

BOIS HUGO   CHALET WOOD   HILL 70

Looking up the slopes of Hill 70. On 26 September the Scots held positions near the summit of the hill, while the Germans held the two woods.

BOIS HUGO   CHALET WOOD

Six battalions of 21st Division were decimated by machine guns hidden in the two woods as they advanced up the hill.

Rifles and 7th KOSB pursued the Germans up the slope heading for the Lens road. Behind the fencing to the left of the track is the site of the Chalk Pit **(A)**. It is still a chalk pit, but has grown in recent years, swallowing up much of the slope. At the end of the track turn right onto a dirt track **(2)**, following the line of electricity pylons. Loos valley is to the right with the Grenay Ridge beyond, the village is directly in front. 44 Brigade advanced up the slope to the left, passing over the summit of Hill 70 (the water tower stands above). To observers across the valley the advance had "the appearance of a bank holiday crowd".

Turn left where the dirt track meets a tarmac road, up the slope **(3)**. It is now possible to view Chalet Wood, in front of which stands a large brick building. On the morning of the 26th this slope witnessed tragic scenes. The Scots were dug in near the summit of Hill 70 when the Germans counterattacked through Chalet Wood and Bois Hugo. The shattered men of 63 Brigade came streaming down the hillside, just as 64 Brigade were preparing to advance from the foot of the slope. The 14th and 15th Durham Light Infantry, fearing they were being attacked, fired on the retreating men. After order was restored the Durham men continued to advance towards the summit of the hill. The Germans in the two woods were presented with a target that was impossible to miss. With the premature charge of the two KOYLI battalions the slope was soon strewn with prone bodies, some alive, many dead or wounded. With the rest of the attack in full retreat from the 'Field of Corpses', 64 Brigade began to retire, leaving the Scots clinging to their trenches near the top of the hill. Continuing up the hill to

On 27 September 2 Guards Brigade tried in vain to reach Puits 14 bis and the two woods.

the T junction: where the houses begin **(4)**, it is possible to take in the full view of Puits 14 bis, Bois Hugo, Chalet Wood and Hill 70.

The following afternoon the Guards Division performed a two pronged attack towards the Lens road. Although the chalk pit has obliterated the ground where 2 Guards Brigade came to grief, it is possible to follow their route across the Loos valley. Nearly 4,000 men, marching in quick time, came over the Grenay Ridge north of Loos, heading for Puits 14 bis. Every gun available was trained on them as they started to climb the hill towards the mine buildings. Lieutenant John Kipling was mortally wounded in the region of the Chalk Pit. Meanwhile, 3 Guards Brigade climbed the hill from the right, having struggled to find a way through the ruined village.

Return down the slope, retracing your route to your vehicle.

Walking Tour 4 - Bois Hugo, Chalet Wood and Hill 70

Heading in the same direction, turn right onto the Lens - La Bassee highway heading south. As the road climbs the hill, turn left by the disused mine buildings at the new roundabout **(5)**. Park your vehicle in the car park on the left. The Field of Corpses is north of the wood. Walk alongside the road, which follows the northern edge of the wood heading towards the aerodrome buildings **(6)**. Before long a fine panorama of the area comes into view. To the left is the La Bassée road, and the reverse slope of the Grenay Ridge beyond. Directly in front, in the distance, is Hulluch village and across to the right are the two copses that mark Stutzpunkts III and IV.

As darkness fell on 25 September, 2 Brigade reached Bois Hugo, and they spent an uneasy time digging in. Meanwhile 1 Brigade held a line to the west of Hulluch; the gap between the two halves of the division was huge. Later that night 63 Brigade took over the perimeter in and to the north of Bois Hugo. At

The Field of Corpses seen from Bois Hugo, Hulluch is at the bottom of the slope.

day break the Germans attacked through the wood, and in the chaotic battle that followed 63 Brigade was routed, falling back past the mine buildings to the right. Around midday on the 26th the fields in front were filled with the men of 72 and 71 Brigades advancing from left to right. The 9th East Surreys crossed the ground directly in front, all the time under enfilade fire from the wood behind. The 8th Buffs, followed by the 9th Suffolks, crossed the lower ground beyond.

Walk back to the main road, and follow the footpath up the hill, alongside the busy Lens road. The wood in front, to the left of the road, is Chalet Wood. Lieutenant-Colonel Douglas Hamilton and his Cameron Highlanders repeatedly charged into the wood on the morning of 26 September. About 300 metres up the hill there is a large brick building to the left, a crematorium **(7)**. It stands in front of Chalet Wood. With your back to the wood it is easy to see how the Germans could enfilade 64 Brigade as they advanced up the slope. Meanwhile, the Scots, dug in near the summit to your left, watched the spectacle unfold. Carrying on up the slope, there is a small concrete shelter in the field to your right,**(B)** ideally placed to observe the Loos valley.

A further 300 metres on and the summit of Hill 70 is reached **(8)**. The area has nearly all been covered by modern buildings now, and the slopes where 46 and 44 Brigade, became pinned down have disappeared under industrial estates. Even so the view to the north east shows how significant the redoubt was. In 1915 the redoubt consisted of two parts, the perimeter trench ran in a semi-circle around the edge of the flat topped summit. The Scots, and later the Guards, dug trenches on the slope beyond the crest **(C)**. The heart of the redoubt, a smaller affair, was centred on the crossroads, positioned to catch anybody advancing across the flat summit.

On 25 September the Scots came over the summit, the Germans fleeing before them. The majority wheeled right, heading south down the main road into Lens, where their route was barred by the German Second Line. Others headed east, chasing Germans towards Cité St Auguste. When it was obvious that there was no way forward, Lieutenant-Colonel Sandilands ordered Sergeant Tommy Lamb to wave the Cameron Highlanders flag to recall them. As the Scots fell back, the Germans followed, charging up the slopes and onto the redoubt. During the ensuing fight Second Lieutenant Johnson VC led his engineers, rallying the infantry around him. By nightfall the Germans held the summit, while the Scots dug in beyond the crest.

To visit the site of the British trenches, cross the road by the traffic lights, taking great care at the busy junction. Heading west towards Loos, walk along the road and between the houses. The Scots dug in on the open slopes to the left and right of the road **(B)**. If you continue down the hill towards Loos a little way **(9)**, it is possible to look across the fields to the left where the Scots line ran. The end of Loos Crassier is hidden among the bushes below the pithead tower. On the morning of the 26th, 45 Brigade's charge onto the summit was driven back. A further assault by the 10th Green Howards and the 12th Northumberland Fusiliers also failed to carry the redoubt. It is important to remember that the area around the crest was completely open in 1915, and the

German machine-guns were able to sweep the summit with their bullets. After the two attacks, Private Dunsire VC made several sorties to rescue wounded men in the field to the right of the road.

Turning round, retrace your route. On the afternoon of the 27th a final attempt to clear the redoubt was made by 3 Guards Brigade. The Welsh Guards advanced to the right of the road while two companies of the 4th Grenadier Guards moved up the slope to the left. Neither were able to enter the redoubt. Return to the summit of Hill 70, then walk back down the La Bassée road to your car.

Walking Tour 5 - Hulluch and the Field of Corpses

From the car park, return to the main road, turning right, heading north for La Bassée. After a mile, take the turning right at the bottom of the slope, sign posted Hulluch **(1)**. After the first few houses, where the road swings left, take a sharp right **(2)**. Park, making sure not to obstruct any properties. For a few hours on the morning of 25 September Hulluch was empty and wide open for exploitation. Although a handful of stragglers entered the village, without reinforcements they were forced to withdraw when German troops arrived. Walking away from the village, it is possible to view the area from the German point of view. Bois Hugo, with the aerodrome building in front, covers the southern horizon. To the right, beyond the Lens highway, is the Grenay Ridge. The German line ran around the tip of the village from the north, before heading east, skirting what is now a wooded area.

At 11.00am on 26 September 1915, line after line of men came over the ridge moving right to left across the highway (see Map 28, p135). The 11th Essex and part of the 2nd Welch advanced across the field in front, by-passing the village. Heavy enfilade fire forced them to take cover in a sunken lane, where the line of bushes is. Changing direction to advance towards the village, a few men managed to enter the German trench east of here. The break through could not be sustained, even though there were few Germans to resist them.

Follow the tarmac track for 300 metres, turning left onto the tractor trail **(3)**, following the line of bushes. As you look to your right imagine in the region of 6,000 men coming over the horizon, and crossing the road into a hail of bullets and shrapnel. With the Germans to the left, right and in front the two brigades of 24th Division stood no chance on the open moor. The Essex and the Welsh took cover along this track before turning to face Hulluch. The Royal West

The view south from Hulluch village, Bois Hugo lines the horizon.

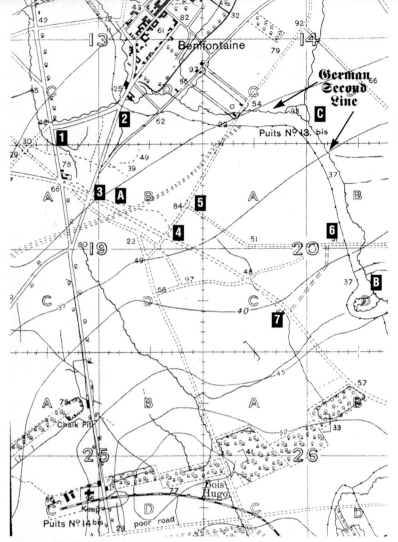

Map 37. Walking Tour 5 - Hulluch and the Field of Corpses.

Kents followed by the Queens advanced to the right of the track, heading east, with the Buffs to their right.

After 300 metres take the track to the left **(4)**, and 200 metres further on take the track to the right **(5)**. The larger group of bushes in front stands near the site of Stutzpunkt IV **(B)**, on the line of the German Second Line. A second smaller group, to the left, is close to Stutzpunkt III **(C)**, where the German trench turned west. Making your way across the fields the all round view is dramatic, and it is easy to see how vulnerable the New Army men were. In front of the bushes the track forks **(6)**; looking back towards the Grenay Ridge it is possible to understand how much 72 and 71 Brigades achieved. By midday on 26

Looking back to the Grenay Ridge from the German positions.

September the whole area between Hulluch and Bois Hugo was littered with prone men, the 8th Queens and 8th Royal West Kent to the right and the 9th East Surreys to the left in front of the wood. The 8th Buffs and 9th Suffolks were pinned down on the ground to your front. During the retirement Sergeant Arthur Saunders VC, nursing a serious leg wound, commanded two machine-guns, near here. By doing so he kept the Germans at bay, allowing many to escape. When the threat had subsided, the German medics emerged to help the wounded, a merciful act considering the carnage that had gone before.

Take the right fork, following the track south west towards Bois Hugo. The 9th East Surreys were pinned down here by the Germans holding the wood. At the T junction **(7)** it is possible to see the remaining section of Bois Hugo on the left. It once ran all the way to the Lens road, where Puits 14 mine stands. Turning right, follow the track across the fields, eventually rejoining the track where the tour started.

Walking Tour 6 - Lone Tree and the Grenay Ridge

Turn your car around and head back onto the main La Bassée – Lens Road. Turning right, head up the hill to the roundabout. The area of scrub to the left of the road is where the remnants of 1 Brigade dug in on the morning of the 25th. The small party of Camerons crossed the road here and entered Hulluch, finding it deserted. At the roundabout, turn left and after a mile, the fields open up to the left of the road. St Mary's ADS Cemetery is a short distance further on, on the left **(1)**. Park your car in the lay-by in front of the Cross of Sacrifice.

After taking a walk around the cemetery, take some time to absorb the views that this location presents. The road was IV Corps' boundary, the area to the north was covered by I Corps. The cemetery stands in what was No Man's Land and the British front line ran from north to south about 150 metres to the west. Looking west across the British rear area, the large farm in the middle distance is Le Rutoire Farm, and beyond is Vermelles. On the morning of the 25th the 8th Royal Berkshires advanced through thick clouds of smoke, losing heavily. Many were hit as they tried to claw a way through the German wire, which ran about 100 metres to the east of the cemetery. On 29 September George Coppard carried machine gun ammunition up to the front line. His description of the scene alongside the road that appears in his autobiography *With a Machine-gun to Cambrai* is particularly graphic;

> ...stretching for several hundred yards on the right of the road lay masses of British dead, struck down by machine-gun and rifle fire. Shells

169

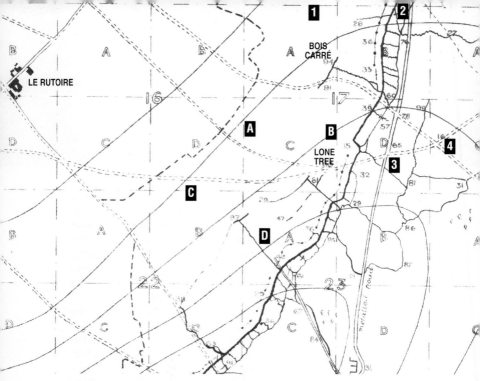

Map 38. Walking Tour 6 - 1st Division's front, Bois Carré and Lone Tree.

from enemy batteries had been pitching into the bodies, flinging them into dreadful postures. As they were mostly belonged to Highland regiments there was a fantastic display of colour from kilts, glengarries and bodies, and also from the bloody wounds on their bare limbs. The warm weather had darkened their faces and, shrouded as they were with the sickly odour of death, it was repulsive to be near them. Hundreds of rifles lay about, some stuck in the ground on the bayonet, as though impaled at the very moment of the soldier's death as he fell forward.

From the cemetery walk east, across what was No Man's Land. By the CWGC signs **(2)**, turn right onto the dirt track. The German support trench ran along side the track, the front line crossed the fields 50 metres to the right. On 25 September the 8th Royal Berkshires lost heavily as they cut through the wire; gassed, shot at and shelled they pushed on across the track and over the

German perspective of 1 Brigade's front, the three cemeteries stand in a line in No Man's Land.

horizon. After visiting the two cemeteries continue south, the 10th Gloucesters advanced from right to left, suffering grievously in No Man's Land. The view across the British rear is spectacular and it is easy to see why the Germans chose to site their trenches on the forward slopes.

Where the track joins from the left **(3)**, stop and take in the view to the right. Lone Tree stood in the fields in front, about 200 metres away. Heading west down the slope, the German front line is crossed after about 100 metres. The 1st Loyal North Lancashires were pinned down just beyond, to the right of the track. Private Henry Kenny VC carried six men across the field back to safety before he was wounded **(A)**. The 2nd Royal Sussex charged forward through the Lancashires, in the hope of breaking the deadlock. Sergeant Harry Wells VC led his men right up to the wire in a desperate attempt to get through **(B)**. The 2nd KRRC advanced to the left of the track, and they too were unable to find a way through the wire. Private George Peachment VC was killed while attending to his officer in the field to the left **(C)**. The Northamptonshires followed and Captain Anketell Read VC led his men across the same field **(D)**.

While 2 Brigade struggled to break though, Green's Force began moving forwards from the direction of Le Rutoire Farm, directly to your front. The 1/9th Kings and 1/14th London Scottish drew attention from every gun in range as they moved across the open. They eventually took cover in and around the trenches that were to your front. By 8.00am the situation was dead-locked and for over three hours nothing stirred, 2 Brigade lay out in No Man's Land, with Green's Force behind. The only brief activity occurred when two companies of the 2nd Royal Munster Fusiliers advanced from the right, having veered off from their intended route through Bois Carré. Around midday Colonel Green's force rose to advance. Without smoke to screen the troops, the advance was doomed and for a second time the situation was a stalemate (See map 9, p56).

Return to the top of the slope and follow the track immediately in front **(4)**. In a few yards the Loos valley opens up, presenting an impressive panorama of the battlefield. Around 3.00pm on the 25th, the 2nd Welch tentatively moved across the slope in front, making their way behind Captain Ritter's force. Seeing the threat to their rear, the Germans surrendered.

Directly in front, at the bottom of the slope, is Hulluch. 1 Brigade held a line facing the village for most of the first day. When 2 Brigade had assembled, the survivors came over the crest to the right and headed into the valley. As night

German view of Lone Tree.

LE RUTOIRE FARM

BRITISH FRONT LINE

Looking east from the Grenay Ridge, 24th Division was decimated as it advanced past Hulluch. The German Second Line ran along the horizon.

approached, they reached Puits 14 bis, the deserted mine buildings at the far side of the valley. From this position you can appreciate the gap between the two brigades. The following morning six battalions moved down the slope, expanding into formation as they went. Crossing the Lens – La Bassée road, that runs from left to right, they were met by a cross fire from left and right. On a clear day it is possible to see the limit of the advance, signified by the two isolated copses on the German Second Line.

After taking one last look over the battlefield, return to your car. Continuing west, head into Vermelles, and at the village centre turn left. Carry on heading south, and out of the village, until the main road between Lens and Bethune is reached. If you intend to return to Bethune to find a place to stay, or just visit, turn right and follow signs for Centre Ville. If, however, you wish to make your way back to the motorway, turn left. After a while, Dud Corner Memorial, your starting point, is passed. The junction for the A21 motorway is clearly sign posted as you climb the far slope of the Loos valley.

Chapter Fourteen

CEMETERIES ON THE BATTLEFIELD

Dud Corner Cemetery and Memorial

The Loos Memorial to the Missing stands alongside the main highway between Bethune and Lens, on the crest of the Grenay Ridge. The walls of the memorial surround Dud Corner Cemetery, a large concentration cemetery built after the war when the area was cleared. They are built on the site of the Lens Road Redoubt, the strongpoint stormed by the 9th Black Watch on 25th September. After the battle the battalion buried its dead here, Lieutenant-Colonel Henderson, Captains Graham and Bell, Second Lieutenant Miller and over 40 other ranks. After the war this site was chosen, due to its central position on the main road, for the Loos Memorial. Nearly 1,800 graves were moved here from the surrounding battlefield. Almost two-thirds of the graves are unidentified although many would have died in September 1915. Around 200 of the identified graves bear the date 25 September 1915.

After the war there were plans to construct a memorial in the centre of

Loos Memorial to the Missing and Dud Corner Cemetery.

Map 39. Commonwealth War Graves Cemeteries in IV Corps area.

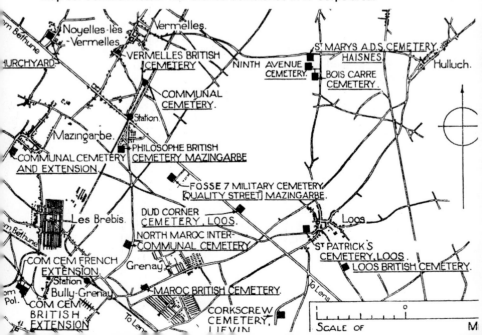

Inauguration of the Loos Memorial.

Bethune, along the lines of the Menin Gate. However, the French authorities raised their concerns over the size and number of memorials proposed. With some under construction, several plans had to be shelved, including the one planned for Bethune. As a compromise it was agreed to build memorial screens around two planned cemeteries. Men who died before the Battle of Loos are remembered on the memorial at Le Touret. The walls surrounding Dud Corner Cemetery bear the names of the men who died in the area between 25 September 1915 and the Armistice. During the construction works the Black Watch 'other ranks' graves were relocated to Philosophe British Cemetery.

The names are inscribed in order of regiment and rank, starting to the left of the entrance. In total 20,712 officers and men are remembered on the tablets, although several graves have been identified over the years. One of these is Lieutenant John Kipling, only son of Rudyard Kipling, of the 2nd Irish Guards. Kipling's grave is situated in St Mary's ADS Cemetery.

The names of three holders of the Victoria Cross are carved on the panels. Lieutenant-Colonel Douglas-Hamilton VC led the 6th Cameron Highlanders in the fight for Chalet Wood. Rifleman Peachment VC, 2nd King's Royal Rifle Corps, was mortally wounded while attending to his injured company commander at Lone Tree. Second Lieutenant Wearne of the 11th Essex was awarded the Victoria Cross for leading a raid to the east of Loos in June 1917. The Germans tried to outflank the intruders as the soon as the Essex men began consolidating their new position. Wearne leapt out of the trench and ran along the parapet throwing bombs and shooting at the Germans below. Although wounded twice during the suicidal attack Wearne continued until killed. Private Bowerman of the 1st Queen's and Private Foulkes of the 1/10th Manchesters were executed for desertion, their names also appear on the panels.

Captain Read VC, of the 1st Northants and Sergeant Wells VC of the 2nd Sussex are buried in the enclosed cemetery. Both were awarded the highest award following the attack at Lone Tree on 25 September 1915. Captain Read's grave is situated in Plot VII, Row F; Sergeant Wellís is located in Plot V, Row E.

174

St Patrick's Cemetery.

St Patrick's Cemetery, Loos

The village of Loos has two military cemeteries. St Patrick's Cemetery is situated opposite the village school. The school is named after Emiliene Moreau, the Angel of Loos who assisted Scottish medics during the battle. The original irregular shape of the cemetery has been maintained as houses have been built around it. The random nature of the graves contrasts with the many concentration cemeteries in the area. The French took over the sector east of the village after the Battle of Loos and French and British First Aid posts worked side by side in the ruined buildings throughout the winter. The 16th (Irish) Division arrived in the area in March 1916 on its first tour of the front line. Each battalion laid out its own plot at the north end of the cemetery. They medics were particularly busy during April and May 1916 when the Germans carried out several gas attacks designed to coincide with the Easter Rebellion in Dublin. The largest group belongs to the 6th Battalion, Royal Irish Rifles.

Two medics of the 150th Field Ambulance were buried in the village cemetery across the road in May 1940.

Loos British Cemetery

Loos British Cemetery, originally known as Loos Provisional Cemetery, is situated on the eastern side of the village. It stands on the site of the Chalk Pit where the 1/20th London suffered many casualties on 25th September. Chalk Pit Copse, a thin strip of woodland that ran along the contour of the slope, was across the road from the cemetery entrance.

The original wartime cemetery was tiny in comparison to what we find today. In the summer of 1917 the Canadian Corps stationed a field ambulance here and rows A and B of Plot I, and the first Row of Plot II, less than 100 graves, were made. These graves are situated at the top of the slope to the right of the gate. Over 2,750 graves were brought in after the war when Loos was cleared. Plots I to XVII contain 2,175 graves and less than ten percent are fully identified. Most of the identified graves date from September 1915. The grave of Major Bill Casson, who led the attack on the Double Crassier, is situated in the second row of Plot VIII. Nearly 400 graves bear the Maple Leaf; these men died fighting on Hill 70 during the summer of 1917.

Loos British Cemetery.

A wide lawn separate the final three plots from the rest; the Cross of Sacrifice and the Stone of Remembrance stand at the centre of the lawn. Most of the graves in these final plots came from smaller cemeteries and many are fully identified. Barts Alley Cemetery, Cauldron or Red Mill Cemetery, Corkscrew Cemetery and Loos (Fort Glatz) Cemetery are just a few of those cleared. Again a large number date from the Battle of Loos. There are two graves dating from the Second World War in Plot XVII, Row G.

St Mary's ADS Cemetery

St Mary's ADS Cemetery stands alongside the road from Vermelles to Hulluch. An advanced dressing station (ADS) was established in the old trenches after 25th September. It contains nearly 1,800 graves, of which only ten percent are fully identified. The majority died in September and October 1915. Many bodies were identified by regimental badges or 'pips' on the tunics. The Buff's, Kings Royal Rifle Corps, Devonshire's and Royal Sussex, who led the assault either side of the road, are particularly well represented. Twelve special memorials to the left of the War Stone remember seven officers of the 10th Gloucesters and five of the 1st Loyal North Lancashires. They were all killed in action on the 25th of September 1915, and they are known to be buried in the cemetery.

The grave of Lieutenant John Kipling, Rudyard's son, stands in Plot VII. The death of this young officer influenced the appearance of the CWGC's memorials and cemeteries across the world. On his seventeenth birthday Rudyard Kipling escorted his son to the local recruitment depots, but poor eyesight prevented John from being enlisted. In desperation, Rudyard contacted Lord Roberts, Colonel in Chief of the Irish Guards (a regiment he privately despised) and obtained a commission for his son. After a year of training John was drafted to France in the 2nd Battalion, which had been assembled ready to join the new Guards Division. Five weeks later, on 27 September, John Kipling was posted missing, presumed dead. Extensive questioning, in part sponsored by his father, revealed that he had become detached from his company during the attack on Puits 14 bis and swept along by the Scots Guards advance.

Rudyard Kipling was haunted by the death of his only son's untimely death until the end of his life. He wrote the following epitaph;

My son was killed while laughing at some jest, I would I knew

What is was, and it may serve me when jests are few.

After the war Kipling became heavily involved in the work of the War Graves Commission and was very influential in the policy of marking the graves of

St Mary's ADS Cemetery.

unknown soldiers. In particular Kipling chose the inscription 'There name liveth for evermore' for the Stone of Remembrance and the words inscribed on the graves of unknown soldiers. When parliament voiced their concerns over the cost of building extensive cemeteries and memorials in May 1920, Kipling addressed a large number of MPs who had served in the war to rally support:

You see we shall never have any grave to go to. Our boy was missing at Loos. The ground is of course battered and mined past all hope of any trace being recovered. I wish some of the people who are making this trouble realised how more than fortunate they are to have a name on a headstone in a named place.

In the post-war years Kipling began writing a history of the Irish Guards, and in 1923 his two-volume work was published. Rudyard made several trips to France to oversee the early stages of the Commission's work. During the trips he and Carrie, his wife, spent many hours visiting cemeteries in the hope of finding their son's grave. Their searches were in vain and Rudyard died a broken man in January 1936.

In 1992 the Commonwealth War Graves Commission received evidence that an 'unknown grave' in St Mary's ADS Cemetery could be that of John Kipling. An investigation led to Plot VII, Row D, Grave 2 being given a new headstone inscribed with John's details. There are some who object to the decision; the evidence briefly is as follows.

The Irish Guards only made one tour of the Loos sector during the war, in the autumn of 1915. During that period three officers of Lieutenant rank died, Lieutenant Hines died of wounds in Vermelles Dressing station and was buried in the Military Cemetery. Second Lieutenant Clifford was posted missing following the attack on 27 September. During the post war clear up, many graves from the battle were identified by items of clothing in particular badges or in the case of officers, metal pips or stars on their tunics. (Metal identity tags did not appear until 1916). The grave in St Mary's ADS Cemetery was originally marked 'A Lieutenant of the Irish Guards'; so by a simple process of deduction the grave must be John Kipling's.

Lieutenant John Kipling's grave.

The debate revolves around the date of Kipling's promotion to full lieutenant. It is known that he had not received formal notification of the commission. Some reason that he was aware of the forthcoming promotion and had sewn the new 'stars' on his tunic before going into battle. Others argue against the proposal. Draw your own conclusions, what is important is that these young men gave their lives and deserve to be remembered without controversy.

After the war the French built their own cemetery across the road. The remains of 800 poilu's who died during the early months of the war were brought here from all over the battlefield. In 1922 the cemetery was closed and the graves moved to Notre Dame de Lorette National Cemetery.

Ninth Avenue Cemetery

Between the 25th and 29th of September the 1st Battalion Cameron Highlanders buried Second Lieutenant Thomas Perry and 41 men in a mass grave alongside a trench known as Ninth Avenue. The trench was dug across No Man's Land to connect the two original front lines. The majority of the Camerons lost their lives on the 28th during an enforced lull in the fighting brought about by a need to reorganise the line. Now the headstones form a square around the grave.

Bois Carré Military Cemetery

Four officers of the 8th Battalion Royal Berkshires, the battalion that led the assault across this part of No Man's Land, were buried together here after the battle. Captain Wilfred Oldman, Lieutenant Hugh Cassels and Lieutenant William Haynes are buried together in Row A, Lieutenant Harold Keable's grave is in Row F. The battalion suffered over 500 casualties on 25th September, many fell victim to machine gun fire as they tried to cut through the German wire. After the Battle of Loos it became a comrades' cemetery, and irregular groups of graves dotted around remind us of this. Well over half of the graves belong to the 16th (Irish) Division, which spent the spring and summer of 1916 holding the line between Loos and Hulluch during its first tour of the trenches. The cemetery suffered considerable damage as the war continued and a quarter of the graves were lost. A long line of special memorials against the far wall of the cemetery commemorates the lost graves.

Bois Carré Military Cemetery.

Vermelles British Cemetery

Vermelles Chateau was used by medical units and the cellars were used to operate on the wounded. The storage cellars of the village brewery performed a similar function.

The first group of graves were laid out by pioneers of the 1st Gloucesters next to a small French plot and for a long time it was known as the Gloucesters

Vermelles British Cemetery.

Graveyard. During the opening stages of the Battle of Loos 7th Division used the cellars for its casualty collecting post. Many of those buried here died from wounds received during the battle. Most of the officers were buried in Plot I.

Plot VI beyond the track to the left of the Cross of Sacrifice also contains many officers graves from the Loos battle. Three officers are buried close together in Row D. Lieutenant-Colonel Leatham DSO, the 2nd Wiltshires commanding officer, died of wounds received at Gun Trench on 26th September. Lieutenant-Colonel Monteith was the second commander of the Bedfords to be hit, after less than a week in command. Captain Radford DSO, of the 1st Royal Berkshires died of wounds two days later. Major (Temporary Lieutenant-Colonel) Arthur Egerton, the 1st Coldstream Guards commanding officer, is buried in Row G. His adjutant, Lieutenant the Honourable Maurice Browne, son of the Earl of Kenmore, is buried alongside. The two officers were killed in the Chalk Pit by the same shell.

There were nearly 2000 graves at Vermelles Chateau when the last Dressing Station left in April 1917. After the war a further 167 graves were added to complete Plots II, III and IV. Meanwhile, the French graves were moved to the French National Cemetery.

There are eight military graves in Vermelles communal cemetery, all belong to artillery men.

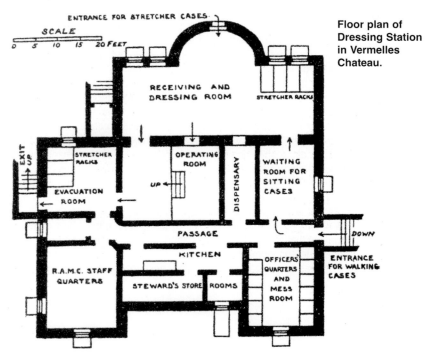

Floor plan of Dressing Station in Vermelles Chateau.

Quality Street (Fosse 7) Military Cemetery.

Fosse No. 7 Military Cemetery (Quality Street)

French troops buried a number of men in the cemetery in May 1915, British troops started at the same time. A few months later 15th Division arrived and many graves belong to Scottish New Army soldiers. In the run up to the battle, the Division's field ambulances took over the houses along the street opposite. The first aid posts were able to deal with 500 men at one time. Splinter proof shelters capable of housing 240 casualties were dug into Fosse 7, the slag-heap to the south.

The elevated embankment to the right heads towards Mazingarbe, and during the battle the railway line was put to use. Coal tucks, converted to carry wounded, would have been overworked on the first day of the attack. 15th Division suffered over 3,500 wounded in forty-eight hours and many would have been treated here. Captain Walpole, the adjutant of the 9th Black Watch, is buried in Row B of Plot I.

Acting-Sergeant John Raynes VC.

A group of artillery men of A Battery, 71 Brigade, are buried against the rear wall. This small group of graves has a story to tell, one which ended in Acting Sergeant John Raynes receiving the Victoria Cross. On 11 October, 1915, after his gun had been subjected to counter battery fire, Sergeant Raynes, was horrified to learn that his friend Sergeant John Ayres had been wounded. After tending to his comrade, Raynes returned to his gun to return fire. When battery was ordered to 'cease fire' Raynes, with the help of two others who were killed soon afterwards, carried the wounded sergeant to safety. As they reached a dug-out, gas shells started to rain down, and finding that Ayres had lost his gas-helmet, Raynes put his own on the wounded man. Raynes went off in search of another gas-mask; however, on his return he was shocked to find the dug-out in ruins. In spite of the effects of the gas, Raynes dug out two survivors, but Ayres had died in the explosion. The following day the battery was stationed near Quality Street, opposite the cemetery, and several of the houses served as billets. When a large calibre shell demolished the cookhouse, sixteen men, Raynes included, were buried beneath the rubble. Despite his own wounds, Raynes managed to free himself, and took part in the rescue operation that followed. After having his own wounds dressed Raynes returned to duty. The shelling on the 12th was so severe that the battery commander;

> ...was obliged to send away to the dressing-station the whole of the
> personnel at that time with the firing battery. Only seven men survived to
> the end of the engagement.

Sergeant Raynes survived the war, but the effects of his injuries plagued him until the end of his life. He died in 1929, aged forty-three.

The main street, known to the soldiers as Quality Street, leads to the Military Cemetery. During the attacks on Hulluch Quarries, Major-General Wing of the 12th Division stationed his advance report centre on Quality Street. He was killed by shellfire on 2 October while crossing the road and became the third divisional commander to lose his life during the battle. He is buried at Noeux-les-Mines Communal Cemetery.

Major-General Wing.

REAR AREA CEMETERIES

Bethune Town Cemetery is situated in the northern outskirts of the town, near to the Industrial Zone. The military plots, comprising over 3000 graves, are situated at the northern end of the cemetery. Plot 1 was for the officers. Lieutenant Frank de Pass VC, of the 34th Poona Horse, is buried in Row A. De Pass was involved in repulsing several German attempts to breach the Indian trenches. He also rescued a wounded sepoy under heavy fire. He was killed on 25 November 1914 while repairing a damaged sap.

In October 1914 Fabian Ware and Dr Stewart, members of the Red Cross, visited the cemetery. According to Ware they 'found a small number of English graves all with plain but carefully made wooden crosses'. From that day onwards the Red Cross Mobile Unit began recording graves and maintaining them. It was the start of what eventually became the Commonwealth War Graves Commission. Sir Fabian Ware led the Commission from the beginning, eventually retiring after the Second World War.

Rows A to I of Plot III were used to bury the rank and file. During 1915 officers here were buried separately from the men, either in Plot II or at the back of Plot III. Lieutenant-Colonel Lord Crichton-Stuart, CO of the 6th Welch and son of the third Marquis of Bute, is buried in Plot III, Row M. He died of wounds received on Hohenzollen Redoubt.

The grave of CSM Hayes of the 2nd Welch at the end of Row B of Plot III tells a different story. The register states that Hayes died in January 1915 from accidental injuries. He was actually murdered by two of his men. The two perpetrators, Privates Morgan and Price, were executed a month later and buried side by side in the first row of Plot IV. An account of the incident is related in Robert Graves' autobiography, Goodby to All That. Private Bryant of the 10th Cheshires is buried in the last row of Plot VI, he was shot for desertion in October 1917. Alongside is a mass grave of 26 soldiers of the 1/8th Manchesters. Having just completed a tour of the Givenchy sector, the men of 'D' Company, the Manchesters, were marching through Bethune during an air-raid, when five bombs caused over 60 casualties amongst them.

The Casualty Clearing Station left Bethune shortly afterwards in fear of

Bethune Town Cemetery.

future raids and the cemetery was hardly used in 1918. In September of that year Lieutenant-Colonel Lord Thynne DSO, a Member of Parliament and son of the Marquis of Bath, was killed by a shell. His grave can be found in Row L at the back of Plot II.

Several hundred French graves made during the first winter of the war were removed from Plot III in the post war years. Eighty-seven Germans prisoners who died of illness are buried in a separate group, next to Plot II.

Sailly-la-Bourse Communal Cemetery and Extension

Sailly-la-Bourse church still bears scars from the First World War. The French buried over two hundred men in the village cemetery between October 1914 and July 1915. The majority died in the autumn of 1914, during what was known as the 'Race to the Sea'. British field ambulances took over the village in August 1915 in readiness for the forthcoming offensive. They were particularly busy in October 1915, during the later stages of the battle.

Private Carter of the 11th Battalion, Middlesex Regiment was executed for desertion in April 1916. After six days of shelling he and several other men deserted from Vigo Street Trench near Vermelles. Although he was obviously shell-shocked, Carter's previous record of desertion, disobedience and sleeping on duty sealed his fate. Private Carter was only eighteen when he died. His grave is situated in Row O.

The 2/8th Battalion Manchesters started the extension in the spring of 1917 and over the next eighteen months 200 burials were made. Three young Australian airmen died in January 1918 when their planes collided during training; they are buried together in Row E. Pilot Officer Edwards, an air gunner with 40th Squadron, RAF, was buried in the Extension in May 1940. His grave is situated in Plot I, Row O.

Labourse Communal Cemetery

Labourse village was used by 7th Division's main dressing station during the Loos Offensive. The communal cemetery is situated to the west of the village. It is a typical ramshackle affair, surrounded by a high wall, the old slag heaps on the skyline complete the gloomy atmosphere. Three men buried in the small British plot were executed for desertion. Private Harry Martin of the 9th Essex and Private Thompson of the 11th Middlesex were shot on 20 March 1916. Private Beverstein died a month later. Fifty French graves dating from the first winter of the war are situated behind the British plot.

Noeux-les-Mines Communal Cemetery

By the time the British arrived in June 1915, over 700 poilus had been buried in Noeux-les-Mines Communal Cemetery. The village continued to be a major medical centre and dressing stations occupied the mines school, the Mairie and several other municipal buildings. During the Battle of Loos both the 15th and the 47th Division used the village. Bracquemont School, to the south, was taken over by the Advanced Operating Centre, a unit which specialised in treating abdominal wounds.

IV Corps evacuated over 14,000 wounded in three days.

The Communal cemetery consists of two large plots containing nearly 1000 graves. Plot I was started in June 1915, the officers were buried in Row A and Lieutenant Martin Young, the officer who encourged Piper Laidlaw to pipe the 7th KOSB into action, is buried in this row. The rows at the back of the plot are filled with mass graves dating from the Loos Offensive. Rows K and L are made up of the graves of officers and many of them served with 15th and 47th Division. Grave 15 in Row K is that of Major-General Frederick Wing CB, commanding officer of the 12th (Eastern) Division. General Wing's ADC, Lieutenant Christopher Tower, is buried alongside. The grave of Lieutenant Robert Valentine of the 8th Royal Dublin Fusiliers is situated at the start of Row L. Valentine was the inventor of the quick-firing improvement mechanism for the Lewis gun. He died from the effects of gas in April 1916.

Number 7 Casualty Clearing Station arrived in Noeux-les-Mines in April 1917. Many of the men that died at the station were buried in the Cemetery Extension in six small plots in the south-west corner of the communal graveyard. Meanwhile, Canadian Casualty Clearing Stations started Plot II. Many of the soldiers buried here were wounded on Hill 70 in August 1917. Two recipients of the Victoria Cross are buried in the Plot. Private Brown, 10th (Canadians) Battalion CEF was posthumously awarded the cross for deeds carried out on 16 August 1917. During a German counter-attack Brown was sent to the rear to ask for reinforcements. Despite being hit in the arm he made it back, collapsing shortly afterwards due to loss of blood. The eighteen year-old succumbed to his wounds the following day. Brown's grave is situated in Row D. A few days later further attacks threatened the positions of the 2nd (Eastern Ontario) Battalion. Major Learmouth personally led the counter-attacks. Despite being badly wounded the Major stood on the parapet to rally his men; several times he picked up German bombs and threw them back. When he could no longer stand, Learmouth refused to leave the front line;

instead he carried on giving encouragement and advice to his men. Major Learmouth was buried in Row K.

Verquin
To the north west of Noeux-les-Mines. 1st Division set up its Main Dressing Station in the village ready for the battle in September 1915. The churchyard contains two mass graves of 18 men.

Philosophe British Cemetery
The military cemetery in Philosphe stands in the shadow of Fosse 3, an artillery observation post. Philosophe brewery was used as a dressing station by many divisions, in particular the 15th (Scottish) Division during September 1915. Its spacious cellars were capable of accommodating three hundred wounded at a time. This dressing station was set up to deal with the walking wounded, so there are very few graves dating from the battle. The cinder track, connecting the cemetery to the road, was the line of the old railway. The converted coal trucks brought the wounded from the front line dressing stations at Quality Street and Fosse 7.

The first burials were made in Plot I in August 1915, not long after the British arrived. the first major influx of casualties came on 27 April 1916. The 16th (Irish) Division were holding the line north-east of Loos when the Germans launched a gas attack, the men that died from gas-poisoning are buried in Rows C, D, E and F. The Irish Field Ambulances continued to use the cemetery throughout the summer. Nearly 200 graves belong to the 16th Division, half of them belong to the 7th Royal Inniskilling Fusiliers.

In November 1916, Plot II was started along the southern hedge, extending the rows of the original Plot and by September 1917 the cemetery had grown to 1,500 graves. Plot III and Plot IV. During the construction of the Dud Corner Memorial, forty-one graves of the 9th Black Watch were relocated to Philosophe. The men fell during the initial assault on Lens Road redoubt on 25 September; their graves stand in a line in Plot III, Row H.

Philosophe British Cemetery.

Mazingarbe Communal Cemetery and Extension
No.45 Field Ambulance occupied Mazingarbe during the attack of the 15th (Scottish) Division. Many of the wounded arrived on board converted coal

Mazingarbe Communal Cemetery.

trucks, which had been 'borrowed' from the local colliery. These small trucks had been boarded out to carry five stretcher cases at a time. Throughout the battle, orderlies man-handled the trucks to and from the collection post at Quality Street. When they reached the brewery, the men were sorted into categories according to their injuries. Those capable of being moved were taken, either by ambulances or wagons, to the casualty clearing station at Noeux-les Mines. Some were beyond help, and had to be left where they lay. Meanwhile, the walking wounded, the gassed and the shell-shocked were shepherded to Le Saulchoy Farm where they could rest and have their wounds tended. This system of collecting, sorting and processing of the wounded enabled the medics to deal with the men in a methodical fashion, rescuing as many as possible.

Just inside the main gate of the Communal Cemetery are a series of village memorials, commemorating the Second World War, when nine members of the local resistance died; another remembers the fallen of the war in French Indo-China. The CWGC war graves are situated against the north wall of the communal plot, to the left of the entrance. The first four graves belong to officers, including two battalion commanders. Lieutenant-Colonel Allenby died within hours of leading his battalion, the 7th Royal Scots Fusiliers, into the trenches for the first time. Private Dunsire, awarded the Victoria Cross for saving wounded men from the summit of Hill 70, is buried in the Communal Cemetery. He died of wounds in January 1916, after a shell demolished his dug-out.

Mazingarbe became known as a place of execution after the Battle of Loos. Ten men were executed in the village abattoir, the majority for desertion. Private J Graham of the 2nd Royal Munster Fusiliers was the first to face the firing squad. He absconded from his battalion's trenches at Givenchy in January 1915. He was eventually caught ten months later in a Bethune brothel. He was shot four days before Christmas. In February 1916 Private John Docherty of the 9th Black Watch and Private John Jones of the 1st Northants were shot a few days apart. Jones was only twenty-one when he died, leaving a widow and young child. His grave is set apart from the rest of the wartime graves. Private Arthur Dale of the 13th Royal Scots was executed for entirely different reasons. In February 1916 Lance-Corporal James Sneddon ordered Dale to leave an extaminet because of drunken behaviour. Dale left, but returned soon afterwards with his rifle and shot the Lance-Corporal. He was executed two weeks later. Corporal Lewis was the last executed man laid to rest in the Communal section. While billeted in Noeux-les-Mines, Lewis discarded his uniform and absconded. He was arrested soon afterwards near the Nieppe

185

Mazingarbe Communal Cemetery Extension.

Forest and execkuted on 11 March 1916.

Private O'Neil of the 1st South Wales Borderers was the first soldier executed for desertion to be buried in the extension on 30 April 1916, his grave is situated in the front row. Driver Hasemore of the Royal Field Artillery is buried in the row behind. At first he was sentenced to Field Punishment Number One for a relatively minor offence. This involved a soldier being tied to a cart wheel or a post for long periods. Hasemore refused to be tied up and his threatening behaviour and insubordination led to a further trial. Hasemore's disobedience resulted in his being sentenced to death; he was executed on 12 May 1916. Two men buried side-by-side in Row D were shot two days apart in May 1916. Private Thomas of the 2nd Sussex served eleven months for his first offence. Shortly after his release he learnt that his younger brother had been killed in action. This prompted Burrell to abscond a second time and as a persistent offender he was executed. Further along the row is the grave of Rifleman Card of the 20th King's Royal Rifle Corps, executed for desertion on the Somme in September 1916. The final execution came eighteen months later. Private Welsh, of the 8th (90th Rifles) Battalion CEF, deserted during the fighting at Passchendale the previous autumn. His grave is situated in the second row of Plot III. Many of his countrymen killed in the fighting on Hill 70 the previous summer are buried in Plot II.

Maroc British Cemetery

In August 1915 French and British troops set up field ambulances in the shadow of the slagheap known as Fosse 5. The 47th (London) Division took over the burial ground a few weeks later, when this sector came under British control. 1st Division was stationed in this area between February and July 1916 and the 1st Loyal North Lancashires had a particularly distressing stay. Four

Maroc British Cemetery.

members of the battalion were executed for desertion and three are buried here. Private William Hunter of North Shields escaped custody twice while awaiting trial. His corps commander recommended a commuted sentence but Haig declined the request. The twenty year-old was executed at the end of February and buried near the end of Row B in Plot I. Private Wiliam Watts absconded while his battalion was stationed in Mazingarbe. He was one of the few soldiers to make it across the Channel and reach his home in Liverpool. He was subsequently arrested, convicted and executed. Watts' grave is at the far end of Row H in Plot I. The third member of the Loyals, Private James Molyneaux, is buried in the same row, near the central path, he was executed in June 1916.

The Canadian Corps held the sector opposite Lens throughout 1917, and the rear of Plot I contains many graves bearing the Maple Leaf.

After the war the cemetery underwent several changes. The French graves were removed to Notre Dame de Lorette National Cemetery, leaving gaps in Rows B and C of Plot I. Meanwhile, 340 graves Commonwealth graves were moved into Plot I and Plot II. Many belong to the 47th (London) Division, dating from August and September 1915. Two long rows of special memorials remember men who are 'known to be buried' amongst the concentration graves. The memorials alongside Plot III remember soldiers of the 1/6th (City of London Rifles) Battalion. Most of them died in the assault on 25 September.

There are fourteen wartime graves in **Maroc Communal Cemetery**. Half belong to artillerymen of the 47th Division.

Bully-Grenay Communal Cemetery French and British Extension

Bully-les-Mines cemetery is situated on the western edge of the village. The communal plot is a mixture of French, British and civilian graves. Two hundred and forty French puilus were buried here before the British arrived in June 1915. The majority of the British graves form one long line of headstones, but only a handful of graves are from the Loos offensive. The main group belongs to the 23rd Division, which held this sector in April 1916. There are a few graves in the civilian plot behind. Driver James Swaine of the Royal Artillery was executed for desertion in June 1916, having absconded whilst on Christmas leave in England.

The Extension was started in April 1916, but it was hardly used for twelve months. Two men were executed for desertion during this period. Private John Smith was the fourth man of the 1st Loyal North Lancashires to be shot, his is buried in the front row of Plot II. Nineteen year-old Private Elsworth Young of Nova Scotia suffered the same fate in October 1916, his headstone stands in the row behind.

The Arras offensive in April 1917 brought a large influx of casualties into Bully-les-Mines. Plots I and II were quickly filled by the Canadian and 24th Division. Private David Stevenson of the 13th Middlesex was shot in July 1918 for desertion. The men chosen for the firing squad had great difficulty in carrying out the gruesome task and two were charged afterwards for failing to fire their weapons. Stevenson is buried in Plot V. Row G. During the post-war years 168 graves were brought here from the fields east of Grenay.

FURTHER READING

The Battle of Loos is a poor relation to many of the longer campaigns on the Western Front. Apart from specific references in unit histories, there are very few books on the subject and most are out of print. The authoritative work is the Official History (1915, Volume II), and the reprints are available from the Imperial War Museum. The Loos volume is very readable, compared to some of the official works. For those of you wishing to find out more about the background to the battle, the official account is the main source of reference.

The Donkeys, by Alan Clark MP, a history of the BEF in 1915, contains a concise version of the battle. Clark's opinion of the High Command is far more critical than that found in the offical version. Many will be familiar with Lyn MacDonald's books and 1915, The Death of Innocence follows the usual format. The chapter on Loos contains many personal accounts that explain the battle through the eyes of those who took part.

Philip Warner's The Battle of Loos, is written from the same perspective. The book was written following a request in the national press for personal accounts of the battle. As a piece of oral history, Warner's work is excellent; there are many moving accounts of life in the trenches and the experience of battle. It is, however, a confusing book. Many of the pieces refer to later battles and in many cases it is difficult to relate the accounts to actual events.

Hopefully, one day there will be a critical study of the battle to bring it the attention it deserves.

Military Operations, France and Belgium 1915, Volume 2 Brigadier-General J Edmonds, Macmillian 1927. Reprint available from the Imperial War Museum

The Donkeys Alan Clark Hutchinson & Co Ltd – 1961 Mayflower-Dell paperback 1964.

The Battle of Loos 1915 Philip Warner William Kimber & Co Ltd – 1976 Wordworth Editions Ltd – 2000

1915, The Death of Innocence Lyn MacDonald Headline Book Publishing – 1993

INDEX

Mazingarbe 9, 27, 104, 107, 111, 118, 180, 184
Mildren, Lt Col 84
Millerand, Monsieur 32
Mitford, Br Gen 109-110, 125, 127, 129, 134, 137, 139
Moreau, Mademoiselle 70, 160
Murray-Threipland, Lt Col 145, 146, 148
Nickalls, Br Gen 109-110, 118, 120-121
Peachment, Private G VC 51-52, 171
Philosophe 27, 111, 184
Pollard, Brig Gen 48, 49, 52, 54-55, 93, 110
Pollock, Lt Col 125
Prothero, Lt Col 92
Puits bis 11 28
Puits bis 13 127
Puits bis 14 25, 54, 62, 69, 93, 119, 125, 141-143, 145-146, 149, 155, 165, 172, 176
Puits bis 15 27, 75,
Ramsey, Lt Col 55
Rawlinson, Lieut Gen Sir Henry 22, 29, 98, 104, 113, 135, 149
Read, Captain A VC 53-54, 171, 174
Reddie, Br Gen 44, 90, 96
Ritter, Captain 60, 92-93, 171
Romer, Lt Col 129
Sanderson, Col 51
Sandilands, Lt Col 68-69, 97-99, 107, 166
Saunders, Sgt A, VC 139-140, 169
Shewer, Bde Maj 138
Stewart, Col 140
Stutzpunkt III 165, 168
Stutzpunkt IV 134, 136, 165, 168,
Stutzpunkt 69 76
Thomson, Lt Col 64
Thwaites, Br Gen 75, 79
Torrance, Captain 58-59
Tower Bridge 27, 76, 79, 93, 111, 127, 155, 159, 162,
d'Urbal, Gen 21
Vansittart, Lt Col 127, 131

Vermelles 23, 31, 58, 109, 144, 178
Wallace, Lt Col 98, 107
Wallerstein, Br Gen 107, 113-114
Walter, Lt Col 121
Way, Lt Col 105-106
Wells, Sergeant H VC 52, 171
Welwyn Garden City 28, 76, 80, 82
Wilkinson, Br Gen M 62, 71
Wilkinson, Br Gen E 104, 107, 113-114
Williams, Captain 146, 148-149
Young, 2/Lt 60-61